JOHN BAILEY'S FISHING GUIDES

WHERE TO
COARSE
F SH
IN BRITAIN
& IRELAND

JOHN BAILEY'S FISHING GUIDES

WHERE TO
COARSE
F SH
IN BRITAIN
& IRELAND

John Bailey

NEW HOLLAND

First published in 2002 by New Holland Publishers (UK) Ltd
London Cape Town Sydney Auckland

2 4 6 8 10 9 7 5 3 1

www.newhollandpublishers.com

Garfield House, 86-88 Edgware Road, London W2 2EA

80 McKenzie Street, Cape Town 8001, South Africa

14 Aquatic Drive, Frenchs Forest, NSW 2086, Australia

218 Lake Road, Northcote, Auckland, New Zealand

ISBN 1 85974 896 1

Edited and designed by Design Revolution Limited,
Queens Park Villa, 30 West Drive, Brighton BN2 2GE
Project Editor: Ian Whitelaw
Designer: Lindsey Johns
Editor: Julie Whitaker

Index by Indexing Specialists,
202 Church Road, Hove BN3 2DJ

Publishing Manager: Jo Hemmings
Series Editor: Kate Michell
Editorial Assistance: Anne Konopelski, Daniela Filippin
Production Controller: Joan Woodroffe

Reproduction by Pica Digital Pte Ltd, Singapore
Printed and bound in Singapore by Kyodo Printing Co (Singapore) Pte Ltd

CONTENTS

INTRODUCTION

There are several objectives to this short book. Its primary use, I guess, will be to sit in the cubbyhole of your car waiting to be taken out when you find yourself in an unfamiliar part of the United Kingdom with some time for fishing. You'll be able to look at your area and pick the right water. Hopefully, you'll have a great day. You should do, because all these waters have been hand-picked, and every one of them is one of my own favourites or that of a friend whose word I trust implicitly.

Or it could be that you are taking up fishing as a relative newcomer and you just want a few pointers to good waters in your own area and places that are reasonably accessible. Once again, I'm pretty sure you'll find an ideal place – somewhere to fit your level of expertise perfectly. I've tried to include all types of waters – wild, difficult, challenging ones, as well as the new breed of commercial fisheries, generally small waters that are heavily stocked and have great facilities. Okay, they don't set quite as much of a problem as the big, natural lakes and rivers, but you've still got to winkle the fish out, and that isn't always easy.

I've also included as many tips as possible, liberally sprinkled throughout the pages or grouped together in boxes. Sometimes, on a strange water particularly, you just need that slightest of nudges in the right direction. You might be doing nearly everything right, but it's the last few steps that turn potential into actual bites. Also, a few tips breed confidence and without confidence you just won't catch. I don't know why that is, but it's true: once you've settled on a plan that you think is right for the day, give it time to work and pretty soon you'll find your hunch was right. Never dash into a fishing situation: sit back, have a think, look at the water and then form a plan.

Fishing is a brilliant, exciting sport and we owe it to the waters, the fish and the wildlife to make sure we behave in a responsible fashion. This is ever more important as public opinion becomes more and more focused on how we behave. Can I, therefore, suggest the following rules that we should all, beginner and expert alike, attempt to emulate? None of this is revolutionary – just common sense.

Firstly, never drop litter or discarded tackle. Remember especially that nylon line does not break down for years and is always a potential hazard for wildlife unless it is taken home and binned properly. Always clear up any litter you might have left during your own session and why not take with you a bin liner so that you can clear away other people's rubbish as well? A lot of people do this nowadays, and as a result we're getting cleaner and cleaner fisheries.

If you get snagged up and leave a baited hook in a tree or bush, for example, make every possible attempt to retrieve it without jeopardizing your own safety. If you can't do this on your own, try to enlist help from others, particularly the fishery bailiff, who might have a boat for such emergencies. Remember that a baited hook left swinging in a tree is a magnet for any bird.

Choose your swim carefully. Try to avoid places that are rife with overhanging trees and other snags. You are simply going to lose gear and/or hooked fish. Also, keep away from areas where picnickers make a habit of feeding wildfowl. The big concentrations of birds found here make ground-baiting impossible, and there's always the fear that they'll dive down and pick up a baited hook.

Never leave a rod unattended. This can easily result in a fish being snagged or it may even pull your rod in. It's also possible that waterfowl can get tangled in the line or even dive down and pick up your bait with disastrous consequences. So always reel in if you need a break, and don't leave the baited hook swinging from your rod tip.

Make sure that your line is in tiptop condition and check it for any fraying or abrasion. Ensure, too, that your knots are secure. Nobody wants a hooked fish to break free. And make sure that you have a weaker breaking strain hook length than your main line. If a fish does break free, at least it will be towing only a short amount of line.

In carp fishing, there's a certain amount of controversy over the use of bolt rigs. These are acceptable providing the ledger weights can slip free should the carp become snagged. If the line does break, you don't want a carp pulling a fixed lead around the lake.

Think also about your hooks. Try to use barbless hooks when at all possible, or at least hooks with a micro barb or a barb that's flattened down by forceps. Unhooking is much easier, and both fish and accidentally hooked birds will find a barbless hook easier to shed.

When you are fishing, always be aware of water birds in the vicinity, and reel in your rig if you think there's any danger of entanglement. When you're ledgering, submerge the rod tip as deeply as is practical so that the line sinks beneath those webbed feet. Take great care when you are fishing surface baits – bread, dog and cat biscuits and so on. It's very likely that waterfowl will recognise them as food and sometimes they will attempt to eat them. A swan can reach something like three feet below the surface, so if you're fishing a shallow swim, be aware of this and reel in if you think there is any danger of it snaffling your bait.

Always do as you would be done to, and help less experienced anglers with any advice you can give them. It's also good to help that elderly or disabled angler by carrying their tackle to the swim.

Look after yourself, too. Never fish in the vicinity of power lines. Modern carbon-fibre rods and poles make excellent conductors, and remember that your rod doesn't actually have to touch the power line for a shock to occur, as electricity can jump some distance.

If you spot a problem with wildlife, contact one or more of these agencies: the RSPCA on 08705 555999; the Wildlife Hospital Trust on 01844 292292; or the National Swan Sanctuary on 01784 431667. Also, keep your eyes open for any signs of fish dying inexplicably or more obvious signs of pollution. If you sense there is something wrong with the water you are fishing, phone the Environment Agency Hotline on 0800 807060. The work of the Environment Agency is augmented by the Anglers' Conservation Association, which fights vigorously against water pollution. All serious anglers should become members, so phone for details on 01189 714770.

I hope I haven't dismayed you with all these 'dos' and 'don'ts'. As I've said, most of this is just common sense. Go out, enjoy yourself totally, but always bear these simple rules in mind.

Scale

mls   0 10 20 30 40 50 60 70 80 90 100
kms   0 20 40 60 80 100

SCOTLAND

EDINBURGH
GLASGOW

LONDONDERRY

BELFAST

NEWCASTLE UPON TYNE
SUNDERLAND

IRELAND

THE NORTH

BRADFORD LEEDS HULL
MANCHESTER
LIVERPOOL SHEFFIELD

DUBLIN

STOKE-ON-TRENT
DERBY NOTTINGHAM
WOLVERHAMPTON LEICESTER
BIRMINGHAM COVENTRY

LIMERICK

EAST ANGLIA

WATERFORD

CORK

WALES

THE MIDLANDS

CARDIFF BRISTOL

THE SOUTH

LONDON

SOUTH EAST

SOUTH WEST

SOUTHAMPTON

PLYMOUTH

N

COARSE-FISHING SITES
IN THE SOUTH WEST

1. *Porth Reservoir*
2. *Bake Lakes*
3. *Angler's Paradise*
4. *Jennetts Reservoir*
5. *New Barn Angling Centre*
6. *The River Exe*
7. *Bussells Pond*
8. *Oldborough Fishing Retreat*
9. *West Pitt Farm*
10. *Viaduct Fishery*

‘ *Water complexes such as Angler's Paradise show that the South West is clearly determined to force itself on the coarse-fishing map of Britain. For too long, Devon, Cornwall and large parts of Somerset were seen primarily as ground for the game fisherman, with very little opportunity for coarse fishing. Little by little, the balance is being redressed, and whilst the game fishing remains very good, coarse fishers are beginning to sit up and take notice.* ’

MATT HAYES, ANGLING WRITER AND TELEVISION PRESENTER

A ll quite true. For generations, game fishermen have travelled to the far South West for the stunning wild brown trout fishing, small stream salmon and excellent sea trout opportunities. Coarse fishing was generally considered very much a junior partner but over the last few years a whole string of very attractive commercial waters has changed the whole complexion of the area. Obviously, tourism is of huge importance to Devon and Cornwall in particular, and the holidaying coarse angler is much too economically important to be overlooked – hence such outstanding fisheries as Angler's Paradise. However, there are many other waters down there well worth a look. In Cornwall, for example, Boscathnoe reservoir, Bussow reservoir and Porth reservoir are all well worth consideration and hold excellent specimens of all the major species. In Devon, you won't find nicer fishing anywhere than at Squabmoor reservoir and Jennetts reservoir, both holding carp to well over twenty pounds. But for real beauty, why not try Slapton Ley, a quite wonderful nature reserve just seven miles from Dartmouth? You've got to fish the water by boat but the pike and rudd fishing in particular are quite superb.

And if it's river fishing that you fancy, then there is access to much of the River Exe, which holds good stocks of grayling, dace and chub in its lower reaches. There are also some roach, perch and pike. In fact, the exploring angler on both the Exe and tributaries such as the Creedy and Culm can find some really idyllic spots well out of the way of the maddening crowd.

PORTH RESERVOIR – CORNWALL

One of many cracking waters run by South West Water, Porth is a large reservoir at eighty acres, but it still has a very natural feel to it. Above all, this is a big fish venue. The carp are approaching twenty pounds and are growing well. The tench and bream are really very large indeed, with both species approaching ten pounds in weight.

Plenty of small roach, perch and rudd can be caught close in, so it's not simply a water for the specialist. Look, however, for the tench and bream further out and ledger for them with perhaps a cage feeder.

Porth is comparatively open to the wind and don't be afraid of ruffled water. It's always tempting to fish the calm bays, but this isn't always where the fish, especially bream, are found. You'd be surprised at the undertows a wind whips up on an open water like Porth, and bream are looking for food coming towards them in the current. The winds generally tend to be warm, so fishing into them isn't too great a sacrifice.

☀ SEASON – open all the year round. Night fishing is allowed.

✦ TICKETS – these can be obtained from a self-service unit in the car park, but also phone the Newtown Angling Centre on 01736 763721 for further details. Also phone 01837 871565 with general enquiries.

➡ DIRECTIONS – you'll find the reservoir on the A3059 a couple of miles outside the town of Porth on the right. Follow the brown signposts.

⊨ ACCOMMODATION – the Tourist Information Centre in Newquay can supply details of a large variety of accommodation on 01637 854020.

BAKE LAKES – CORNWALL

Bake is a commercial fishery that offers a really good spread of species of all sizes, and caters for all levels of fishing experience. For example, the five-acre specimen lake, Luxor, holds carp just over the twenty-pound mark, bream edging towards double figures and some really good-sized tench. At the other end of the scale, the smaller Treasure Island pond has a really good spread of species up to three or four pounds in weight. So you can fish a float a couple of rod lengths out and end up with roach, bream, carp or tench.

On Luxor, look for the deeper holes, especially close in. Sometimes you'll find drop-offs to twelve feet or more. Conversely, try floating crust early and late for the carp. Maggots, pellets and corn all work well for the tench and bream, but don't over-feed. You will find lots of features – islands, ledges, plateaux and the like – so it pays to do a bit of work with a plummet before actually fishing.

If you're fishing Treasure Island, don't always use very small baits, as there is a large head of gudgeon in the water. Don't forget to take your loaf either: not only is floating crust a good bait, but a knob of flake on a size eight or ten is just right for the tench.

Expect good bags of fish a pound or two in weight. Of all the lakes, Treasure Island, particularly, is generally well coloured, so big bags are possible. However, it's a small water so don't make any unnecessary noise or vibration. Sit well back, bait steadily and build up a going swim.

⚓ SEASON – Bake is open year round. There is a ground bait limit of one kilo on Luxor and half a kilo on Treasure Island. Unhooking mats are also essential at Luxor and can be hired. Carp pellets are allowed, but not trout pellets.

🎣 TICKETS – tickets range from £6 on Luxor to £3.50 for children on Treasure Island. Tony Lister will give all the details on 01752 849027.

➡ DIRECTIONS – from Plymouth, take the A38 towards Liskeard. Go through Landrake and Tideford and in just over a mile you will come to the Trerulefoot roundabout. Go straight on, head for Bake and turn right at the T-junction. Take the next left towards Hessenford. You will find the fishery entrance approximately a quarter of a mile on the right. It is opposite Bake Farm.

🛏 ACCOMMODATION – contact the Tourist Information Centre in Plymouth on 01752 304849 for advice on various kinds of accommodation available in the area.

ANGLER'S PARADISE – DEVON

The designer fishery is now part of the coarse-fishing scene, as it has to be. There simply are not enough 'natural' waters to cater for the huge number of anglers who want to fish. So, the commercial fishery has an increasingly important part to play in the modern fishing scene.

And no designer fishery could conceivably be better planned, more imaginative or more compelling than Angler's Paradise on the fringes of Dartmoor. Zyg Gregorek and his wife Rose created Angler's Paradise on a seventy-acre estate way back in 1985 and since then have set dramatic new standards in the field of commercial fisheries. Zyg has created twelve glorious lakes in this beautiful, rural setting.

And what fish stocks they hold – carp, golden tench, golden orfe, blue orfe, golden rudd, goldfish, catfish, shubunkins, grass carp, koi carp, as well as all the traditional species. Throw in woods full of deer, foxes and badgers, skies teeming with buzzards, barn owls and even kingfisher, and you really start to get the picture. Your angling skills don't matter here; expert or novice, you're bound to find the lakes for your own brand of fishing. There is even a lake where nobody has ever blanked. No, not ever! At the other end of the scale, there are thirty-pound carp to be caught, and record golden tench and orfe.

You stay on site in one of the twenty-plus purpose-built villas. These are beautifully presented and together give the impression of a little Mediterranean village tucked away in the heart of Devon. Add the excellent attractions of this part of the world – the north Cornish coast, the Devon resorts, the old towns of Okehampton and Tavistock –

and you realise that Angler's Paradise offers the perfect family holiday. There's even an African-themed bar where you can all relax in the evening after the heavy job of catching fish is over. As Zyg says, 'So many people rebook before even finishing their present holiday, we know we must be doing something right!'

⌂ **SEASON** – the fishing is year round.

⊨ ⚡ **TICKETS AND ACCOMMODATION** – contact Zyg or Rose at Angler's Paradise, The Gables, Winsford, Halwill Junction, Devon EX21 5XT, or phone 01409 221559 for their comprehensive list of prices. Lakes and villas do vary in price according to the season and availability. From October to March, there are special winter breaks available – in the warm Devon winters, the carp still feed well.

🐟 **RULES** – the only real rule is to enjoy yourself – at the same time, obviously, taking every precaution over the welfare of these wonderful fish. Zyg will certainly advise on the best way to treat the fish stocks.

➡ **DIRECTIONS** – at the end of the M5 motorway, take the A30 to Okehampton. At Okehampton junction, take the B3260 to Okehampton and a mile after Okehampton, take the A3079 to Holsworthy and Bude. Take this road for about eleven miles until you reach the Halwill junction. Take the first right-hand turning past the garage, signposted Angler's Eldorado. Go past the Junction Inn and carry on for half a mile until you come across a signpost for Angler's Paradise.

JENNETTS RESERVOIR – DEVON

South West Water controls an intriguing series of reservoirs, generally set in rolling countryside, that are open to the coarse fisherman. All these waters are very well maintained, with nice stocks of fish. Jennetts is the one that I know the best, and it's a lovely water of about eight acres, with depths going down to some thirty feet or so. For a reservoir, it is very natural-looking and set in a beautiful landscape. The fish, too, are splendid – carp to twenty pounds plus, tench averaging three pounds and good roach, bream, rudd, perch and eels.

All the South West Waters hold good stocks of eels and, for those not used to them, they can make an intriguing addition to a holiday bag. Believe me, a big eel is something to be tangled with – and there are some crackers in this part of the world. There are several golden rules when eel fishing, First, make your rig as resistance-free as possible – eels will drop a bait the instant they feel pressure. Next, make sure that you strike immediately you have a run, especially with a small bait, or you will have a deeply hooked eel, which nobody wants. Thirdly, make sure that you can control the eel while you unhook it with forceps. Barbless hooks help considerably in this respect. Eels are not for everyone, admittedly, but if you haven't caught one before, perhaps you'll want to give them a go.

☀ **SEASON** – open all year round from 6.30 am until 10.00 pm.

⚓ **TICKETS** – on Jennetts these cost £4 a day. Contact the Ranger on 01288 321262 or South West Water Leisure Services on 01837 871565 for details.

➡ **DIRECTIONS** – take the A386 out of Bideford towards Great Torrington. After about a mile you will find the reservoir by the side of the road.

🛏 **ACCOMMODATION** – contact the Tourist Information Centre in Bideford, on 01437 477676, who will advise on various types of accommodation in the area.

FURTHER SOUTH WEST WATER VENUES:
DARRACOTT, NR. TORRINGTON – a three-acre coarse fishery with carp, tench, bream, roach, rudd, perch and eels. Open all year round, twenty-four hours a day.
MELBURY RESERVOIR, NR. BIDEFORD – twelve acres with carp, bream, roach, perch and eels.
LOWER SLADE RESERVOIR – carp tench, bream, roach, rudd, gudgeon and perch,
TRENCHFORD RESERVOIR, NORTHEAST OF NEWTON ABBOTT. Big pike.
For details of all these waters contact the Manager at South West Water Leisure Services, Higher Coombe Park, Lewdown, Okehampton EXE20 4QT, or phone. 01837 871565.

NEW BARN ANGLING CENTRE – DEVON

New Barn consists of four lakes, one of which is very much for juniors, with huge stocks of roach and perch. Mirror Lake, it's fair to say, is the most popular simply because the carp fishing there is so impressive. There are lots of double-figure fish, and a good number of twenty-pound pluses. It's an interesting fishery to say the least, and the carp can be picked up in a number of ways. Floater fishing works, as does float fishing close in and the more conventional boily approach. They're good-looking fish here, and plenty of them.

Willow and Lily Lakes are both great waters and do tend to be somewhat under-fished. Great for the exploring angler, one who is willing to stalk fish and look for carp feeding in the most unusual of places.

There are three more excellent reasons to go to New Barn. The first of these is the cracking roach fishing on offer. Roach in stillwaters can frequently be a bit of a mixed blessing: they often over breed, lose condition and become pretty stunted. But not here. There are plenty of fish well over the pound. Maggot and casters tend to be favourite baits, and obviously pole fishing does sort out some big bags. But don't neglect the waggler, especially when there's a wind blowing. The second reason to go to New Barn is its stunning situation, set in a verdant valley with tremendous views. This is a lovely bit of the Devonshire countryside and a superb place to just sit and meditate. And third? Well, New Barn is a tremendously welcoming place. There's tuition if you want it, along with all the facilities you could ever need, but without losing the natural feel of the place. In short, it's no wonder that the locals patronise it so regularly. A cracking place.

☀ **SEASON** – the fishery is closed from mid November to mid February.

TICKETS – day tickets cost £5 for adults and £3 for juniors – phone 01803 553602 .

➡ **DIRECTIONS** – take the A385 out of Paignton following the signs to the zoo. You will be on the Totnes road. Pass the zoo and travel straight over the Tweenaways traffic lights, still on the Totnes road. You will travel for two miles. The fishery is on the left just after an 'S' bend.

ACCOMMODATION – contact the English Riviera Tourist Board on 0906 680 1268 (premium rate number) for details of accommodation in the whole of this area.

THE RIVER EXE – DEVON

There isn't a huge amount of wild coarse fishing in the South West, and most of it tends to be centred on the commercial fisheries. The River Exe, however, does offer the occasional opportunity, even though it's better known as a salmon, trout and sea trout river and is naturally rather tightly preserved upstream. However, once you get into the Exeter area itself there are more possibilities, largely because of the excellent Exeter Angling Club.

❧ TROTTING FOR DACE ❧

The River Exe offers some enchanting dace fishing. Okay, dace don't grow huge, but they're a delicate and absorbing fish species. Trotting is the way to catch them. A twelve- or thirteen-foot rod, three-pound main line, two-pound hook length and either centre-pin or fixed-spool reel are ideal.

- *You'll need maggots or casters for bait.*
- *A stick float is ideal, set so that the bait skips its way through the swim, just a couple of inches off the bottom.*
- *Look for reasonably quickly-paced swims between three and six feet in depth, preferably over gravel, sand or clean bottom.*
- *Feed the swim steadily, say ten or fifteen maggots each trot down.*
- *Let the float trot some fifteen or twenty yards before retrieving. Retrieve close in to the bank to avoid disturbing the swim.*
- *If you don't contact dace after thirty to forty minutes, move down the river until you do come across fish. It shouldn't take too long before a dace shoal responds to a steady flow of maggots.*
- *Don't keep dace in keep nets, but release them immediately. This won't unsettle the shoal.*
- *Remember that an eight-ounce dace is a specimen in its own right – so admire it and give it the respect it deserves.*

The Exe here has become a tidal river for much of its length, and has lost the clarity and intimacy of its upper reaches. Still, there are some good fish to be had. Bream are a top species in these tidal reaches, and average a very handy three to five pounds with some fish, apparently, approaching double figures. Location is the problem. With a large tidal range, you tend to find that the shoals look for a reasonable amount of water over their heads and stick to the deeper pools. These are better located at low water, when you can build up a clearer picture of the bottom contours. Make a note and stick with these areas even when the tide is up. Very occasionally, you will see fish roll and that, of course, gives the game away!

Most of my own tidal-river breaming has taken place in Norfolk on the Bure and Thurne, and I've learnt that it is vital to keep bait going in. In fact, because of the depth and speed of the water and the number of fish present, it is difficult to overfeed. Of course, getting your feed in accurately is a problem and this is where a big cage feeder pays dividends. Keep working the area pretty tightly and you should start the fish feeding. Go for a big, obvious bait – a hunk of flake is a good idea, or even a whole lobworm on a size six hook. Obviously, maggots and casters do work, but not nearly as well in extremely coloured water – and there's always a risk of bootlace eels.

The tide is also a consideration. In Norfolk, I always like it when there's been a flow on, but high water can also work as well. It's hard to predict exactly how the fish are going to react and this makes for really challenging, interesting sport. I will add finally that brackish-water bream really fight like the clappers. They're not at all like the manure-sack creatures of the stillwaters. Get a six-pounder with an ebb flow behind it, and you really know you're into a fish.

All the usual species are present, including the occasional big carp and chub. However, one of the most interesting things is the invasion of mullet that takes place during the summer months. These will run the river in huge numbers, but they can be absolutely infuriating to catch. They're feeding all right, often throwing up huge sheets of bubbles – but catching them is another matter!

Sometimes you'll even see them grazing on the bankside grasses and reeds, presumably hoovering off minute insects. Breadflake is probably as good a bait as any to catch them. Throw in handfuls of mash and look for fish swirling amongst the floating pieces. A pinch of breadflake on a size twelve hook fished in mid water can sometimes do the trick – I'm not going to say that it will always work, or even often, because there seem to be no rules in mullet fishing as far as I'm concerned, but it can work. All in all, an interesting place to fish.

SEASON – check with the controlling club, as the whole question of the closed season is currently under debate.

TICKETS – day tickets cost £3 for adults and £1.25 for juniors. Contact Exeter and District Angling Association on 01647 24566.

DIRECTIONS – take the B3182 out of Exeter towards Exmouth. Turn right at Countess

Wear roundabout, signposted Torquay. This dual carriageway crosses the Exe after half a mile. You will find a car park on the left a little way further on. Park here and walk to the river.

◄ ACCOMMODATION – contact the Tourist Information Centre in Exeter on 01392 265700 for details of suitable accommodation.

BUSSELLS PONDS – DEVON

I mention these small waters because they're very attractive to fish but, and here's the big thing, they're just four miles from the centre of Exeter, affording a great little fishing adventure for anyone making Exeter their base. And there are some nice surprises, such as the very good-sized bream and tench that you wouldn't expect to get to six pounds plus in waters totalling less than three acres. The carp fishing is the main draw and there are plenty of doubles – I'm not sure about twenties, but time will tell. There are also roach and some quite sizable pike. All in all, a pleasant fishing experience, and only a quarter of an hour or so from the hurly-burly of a major city. A nice idea.

☼ SEASON – open all year round.

✦ TICKETS – these cost £5 – phone 01392 841238.

➜ DIRECTIONS – take the A396 Tiverton Road out of Exeter for about three miles. You will come to the village of Stoke Canon. Turn right at the church, signposted Poltimore. In about half a mile, turn left opposite the Barton Cross restaurant. The fishery is half a mile down that road on the left.

◄ ACCOMMODATION – try Exeter Tourist Information Centre on 01392 265700 for details of suitable accommodation.

OLDBOROUGH FISHING RETREAT – DEVON

I haven't actually fished at Oldborough but I've walked the two waters and found them fascinating. They are not particularly large – both around about the acre, give or take a bit – but they are surrounded by trees, look very natural and, being spring-fed, are very fertile. They're also deep – something that gives an extra dimension to any small stillwater. Fish stocks, too, are good. The carp average double figures and four- and even five-pound tench are the norm. There are some very big perch – don't be surprised by two-pounders – and the roach and rudd are also a good size.

These waters are so intimate that long-range bolt techniques aren't really called for. A fair amount of both waters is also out of bounds and therefore the fish don't get too neurotic and can always go into hiding. Therefore, you've got to use traditional fishing skills to some degree at Oldborough: think about floater fishing or even laying-on under your rod tip. This means that you've got to feed carefully and thoughtfully and gradually get a swim going. All the traditional baits work: if the tench are shy, why not try just half a grain of corn on a size sixteen?

☼ Season – open all year.

✦ Tickets – these must be booked in advance and cost £4 a day, £3 for juniors and senior citizens – phone 01363 877437.

→ Directions – take the A377 north out of Crediton through the village of Copplestone. Turn right at Morchard Road, go up the hill and turn right again at the T-junction. You will find the fishery on the left at the bottom of the hill.

▭ Accommodation – Holiday chalets on site – phone Oldborough on 01363 877437. For other accommodation, try the Exeter Tourist Information Centre on 01392 265700.

West Pitt Farm – Devon

West Pitt Farm is one of the new commercial fisheries that have proved so popular over the past few years, and it really is a beauty. It's the brainchild of owner Rod Crocker, who has developed the four pools into really lovely coarse-fishing waters. Farmyard Pool is, as you'd expect, bordered by the farm buildings themselves, but it has a relaxed atmosphere. In essence, this is an old water, quite shallow, but it holds good stocks of carp, roach and rudd. It's an ideal place to sit and while the day away.

Higher Pool is a newer water, quite small but is nicely mature with good stocks of big bream, tench, roach and some lovely golden orfe. Mallard Pool is quite small – about one and a quarter acres in size – but it holds some beautiful common carp topping the twenty pound mark. Willow Pool is smaller still, but has a very interesting selection of fish species. Tench grow to eight pounds and there are perch and crucian carp over two pounds. There are even a couple of barbel that have found their way in, and now top the three-pound mark.

All in all, West Pitt Farm offers something for everybody. If you want to fish the pole and maggot for small roach and rudd, then you'll catch legions of these all day long. If it's bigger fish that you've set your mind on, there are plenty of specimens available – the perch in particular offer really exciting opportunities. But don't forget those beautiful commons and golden orfe. Lovely waters, lovely landscape and very friendly people all combine to make West Pitt a very desirable fishery.

☼ Season – open all year round.

✦ Tickets – the fishing is free to residents and costs £4.50 for adults. After 5.00 pm, tickets cost £3.50. Contact Rod Crocker on 01884 820296 or fax him on 01884 820818.

→ Directions – West Pitt Farm is only five minutes from junction 27 of the M5 motorway. Take the dual carriageway signed to Barnstaple. After five hundred yards, take the left fork to Sampford Peverell. Almost immediately there is a mini-roundabout where you turn right and cross over the dual carriageway. Go straight over the next mini-roundabout heading for Holcombe Rogus. Take the next left signed Whitnage – following the green fish signs – and the next right, signed Whitnage, to Pitt crossroads. Turn left, and West Pitt Farm is signed about five hundred yards on the left.

ACCOMMODATION – West Pitt Farm offers excellent accommodation on site. Rod Crocker offers a selection of cottages suitable for either individuals, couples or even groups up to nine. There's a modern, indoor, heated swimming pool incorporating a sauna and solarium. Children are catered for with a small but discreet play area. Other facilities include a games room with snooker and table-tennis tables, a grass tennis court, barbecue area and plenty of garden furniture around the lawns and tended grounds in which to relax.

VIADUCT FISHERY – SOMERSET

This is an entertaining complex of small waters, deep in the heart of Somerset, with a tremendous stock of fish. This is the appeal. It isn't particularly a specimen water, but the carp fishing on offer is enough for a fantastic family day out. Indeed, the management realise this and offer shared peg facilities for families – a great idea so that everyone can fish together and join in the fun.

The average run of carp is anything between two and seven or eight pounds – not huge, but they're in great condition, fight well and there are bags of them to catch. Try all the normal methods, especially waggler fishing close in for a real thrill. It is obviously a water where the method feeder works particularly well. The method feeder, as you probably know, is a technique that's sweeping the field on many of these small commercial waters.

The concept behind the method feeder is to present a large ball of ground bait with the hook bait tucked right in. When cast into the swim, the carp simply think that you're lobbing in a loose-fed ball of ground bait and they attack it trying to get the food as quickly as possible. The hook bait is therefore mopped up without suspicion. When you're choosing your feeder you'll be faced with an elasticated one or, better, those that feature a hollow tube through which the line runs. These are safer for the fish because they're not actually tied to the main line, which is an advantage in the event of a main line breakage. The fish can simply swim off without towing the feeder behind it. The trick to the method feeder is mixing your ground bait to the right consistency so that it moulds well and doesn't break off the feeder in flight. Experiment a few times until you get it nice and stiff and clingy.

The other tip is to work as much food as you can into that ground bait, so that the offering is as attractive as possible. Perfect additions include hemp seed, casters and sweetcorn. The problem with maggots and worms is that their wriggling can break up the ground bait in flight. Once the feeder settles, the carp will be on it instantly, sucking and pulling. Ignore odd nudges and tugs and wait for the tip to go right round. You're rarely left in any doubt as to when the bait has been taken! This is a highly effective method for the summer, particularly when the carp are really hungry and looking for large amounts of food. It can still work in the winter, but then you should cast out less frequently and give the fish more time.

Back to Viaduct; you'll also contact the odd bream, tench and roach, but perch are the one real specimen species that swims the waters. Now, a big perch is an unpredictable beast. The waters can be full of them one year, and they disappear like magic the next. So when you hear of a water doing the business with perch, it pays to concentrate on it.

⚘ **SEASON** – open all year. Note that barbed hooks and hooks larger than size twelve are banned. There is no night fishing, and several baits, such as nuts, are also prohibited.

⚔ **TICKETS** – available on site for £5 a day and £4 for juniors – phone 01458 74022.

➜ **DIRECTIONS** – take junction 23 off the M5 and head along the A39 towards Glastonbury. Just before Glastonbury, turn right onto the B3151 and you will come to the village of Somerton. The fishery is well signposted to the north of the town.

⊨ **ACCOMMODATION** – the Tourist Information Centre in Glastonbury, on 01458 832954, or Yeovil, on 01935 471279, can advise on accommodation in their areas.

❧ HIGHLY RECOMMENDED FISHERIES ❧

* *Coombe Water, Kingsbridge, Devon. A three-lake complex holding good carp, roach and bream. The carp average five to ten pounds, there are some good roach. Tickets cost £5 a day. Phone 01548 852038.*
* *Emerald Pool, Highbridge, Somerset. A really good carp venue with fish around the twenty-pound mark and some very good roach. Popular with matches so check on availability beforehand. Phone Alan Wilkinson on 01278 794707.*
* *Elmfield Farm, Launceston, Cornwall. A really popular venue. Some excellent carp and roach to over two pounds. Superb fish indeed. Good bream, some chub and perch. Phone 01566 781243 for details and directions.*
* *Slapton Ley, Dartmouth, Devon. A beautiful, natural fishery holding pike, rudd, roach, eels and perch. Part of a national nature reserve. Boat fishing only. For tickets contact The Field Centre, Slapton, Kingsbridge, TQ7 2QP, or phone for further information on 01548 580685.*

Coarse-Fishing Sites in The South

N

Malmesbury
Swindon
M4
BERKSHIRE
Marlow
Maidenhead
River Thames
Slough
Chippenham
Windsor
A346
A4
Marlborough
Hungerford
A338
Newbury
7
Reading
Bracknell
Melksham
M4
5
River Kennet
6
Devizes
Kingsclere
WILTSHIRE
A350
Salisbury
Plain
Basingstoke
M3
8
A331
Aldershot
Warminster
Amesbury
A36
Andover
HAMPSHIRE
Alton
A303
A338
River Test
M3
A31
A3
Salisbury
Winchester
A36
Shaftesbury
Romsey
4
Eastleigh
Petersfield
Sherborne
Blandford
Forum
A354
Ringwood
A31
New
Forest
Lyndhurst
SOUTHAMPTON
M27
Fareham
A3(M)
Havant
DORSET
Gosport
Portsmouth
Bridport
A37
Dorchester
A35
Poole
1
2
Cowes
Ryde
Wareham
Bournemouth
Christchurch
Freshwater
Newport
ISLE OF WIGHT
Lyme Bay
Chesil Beach
Weymouth
Swanage
Poole Bay
3
Sandown
Shanklin
Fortuneswell
Bill of Portland
ENGLISH CHANNEL

❝Yes, John, I'd really try to get down to the Hampshire Avon if I were you. The Royalty's the place to begin probably because there's so much information on it and you can see the fish there. Whoppers. There are definitely chub to over six pounds, and goodness knows how big the barbel go to. Also there are good roach, perch, even some cracking bream. The trend these days seems to be to fish small baits for the barbel, but my advice to you would be to go for a big natural. Try a couple of lobworms or a small dead gudgeon perhaps, and look out for fireworks. It's really liquid history down on the Royalty you know. There have been so many great anglers, so many amazing captures... a man like you starting out on a big fish career just can't ignore it. ❞

A LETTER FROM THE LATE RICHARD WALKER TO THE AUTHOR

As a boy, there was one Mecca that I and my fishing friends all aspired to fish. One day, we told each other, we would fish the Hampshire Avon. The Royalty. The place where Richard Walker, Fred Taylor, Mr Crabtree – heroes real and fictional – all said the biggest coarse fish in England were to be found.

Since those early days, I have fished the Royalty and, though it may not be the river it once was, it's still exceptional. And that goes for many southern rivers. They have had their problems, but there are still some extraordinary fish to be taken. The Stour, the Kennet, the Avon – even smaller rivers like the Allen – can all still produce leviathans.

As Phil Humm, the well-known Essex fisherman, recently told me; 'The southern rivers still hold very, very big roach, and in places they are still present in numbers. I remember one particular swim a year or so ago. It was dusk and there were roach – really big roach – just rolling everywhere. Fishing for them wasn't easy. It never is with roach, but that's not the point. Those southern rivers can still do it'.

Of course, there are also lovely lakes – Broadlands springs to mind. Large carp, tench, pike – you name it, the southern counties hold them.

THE ROYALTY – HAMPSHIRE

For river fishermen, the Hampshire Avon has been their Mecca for decades. And on the Hampshire Avon, no other fishery is as famous as the magnificent Royalty. What a place! It's been glorified ever since the 1930s with strings of extraordinary catches – chub, barbel, roach, pike, perch. For most of the 20th century, the Royalty was the place that all river anglers dreamt of visiting. It became part of angling folklore, back in the 1950s, through Mr Crabtree, who made it appear that every cast would result in a six-pound chub.

Of course, I can't comment on what the Royalty was like in the mid part of the 20th century, as I only came to it properly in the 1980s, when it was still awe-inspiring but definitely difficult. Of course, the Royalty wasn't alone in experiencing hard times. All lowland rivers were having problems. Disastrous river management techniques had had a detrimental impact on rivers throughout all the English counties, and the Avon was not exempt. In fact, much of the upper Hampshire Avon had become even more difficult than the Royalty. The huge roach that once lived there had all but become a distant memory.

The situation today, at the start of the 21st century, looks definitely brighter. The Royalty is once again performing well. Looking back to 1998, there were over 140 double-figure barbel caught from the Royalty alone that season, with vast numbers of barbel under three pounds also being caught. Today, those smaller fish are coming through well, and it's possible to see groups of barbel nudging the five-pound mark. These are going to provide great sport for the future.

The Royalty is a strange beast; such is the glamour of its crystal-clear, characterful waters that you tend to forget it's an urban river only five minutes from the centre of Christchurch. Yes, if your concentration wasn't so fixed on the water, you would be aware of traffic, pedestrians and the ugly sounds of civilisation. But as it is, the only world that exists for you is seen through your Polaroids. Such famous swims – the Pipes, Parlour Pool, the Top Weir, Bridge Pool – all places that have settled into angling folklore. In fact, one leading angling paper voted the Royalty as the best day-ticket river fishery in the entire country. We've already discussed the barbel that easily top twelve pounds – didn't Chris Yates stalk a fish in the Parlour Pool for a number of years that he swore was fifteen plus? There are seven-pound chub, perch over two pounds, big bream and carp, and pike weighing over thirty pounds.

Mind you, just because the Royalty is stuffed with big fish, it doesn't mean to say that you're going to catch them. You'll certainly see these whoppers, but that could well be all! So, how about a few tips.

Firstly, don't use line less than eight pounds breaking strain – if you do hook a fish you want to land it. Secondly, master the art of rolling bait. The barbel at the Royalty have become very suspicious of static ones. And thirdly, show a little inventiveness when it does come to baits – don't just use the same old luncheon meat. How about a couple of lobworms or a small dead minnow?

Try baiting a swim up on arrival and then leaving it a couple of hours to see if barbel have moved in and begun feeding. The longer you leave a swim, the greater the confidence of the fish becomes.

Never neglect to wear your Polaroids. Without them, your ability to see into the water is vastly reduced and your chances of success plummet. And travel light. The Royalty is not the place for bivvies, bolt-rigs and bite alarms. A wealth of tackle might increase your confidence initially but it won't help you catch barbel, I promise.

⚛ BARBEL BASICS ⚛

Barbel are arguably our most dramatic freshwater fish, and certainly very much the target species of the moment. However, catching these magnificent fish can be a difficult business.

There are two basic approaches to barbel fishing. You can either fish at a known peg and put in a lot of bait, building the swim up, or you can travel light and fish as many swims as possible, hoping to pick fish up as you go. Remember that the best times for barbel fishing are dawn and dusk, just into darkness. But that does not mean that they cannot be caught during the day, even in bright weather.

- *Top baits are maggots, casters, sweetcorn, lobworms, dead minnows, luncheon meat, meatballs and garlic sausage. The important thing to remember is to ally the bait to the right size of hook.*
- *Hemp seed is a great barbel attractor. It certainly gets them feeding, but it can preoccupy them with the tiny seeds and make catching difficult. Use it thoughtfully.*
- *You can either ledger for barbel with a lead or a swim feeder or you can float fish. Float fishing is especially useful when the barbel have been very pressurised and are afraid of static baits.*
- *If you're not attracting bites, never be tempted to scale your tackle down in strength. What's the point of moving to three-pound hook length for it only to be smashed in seconds?*
- *A quiver tip and swim feeder set up is probably the most common method used in barbel fishing today. Don't always expect a huge pull round. Barbel bites can often be a mere flickering of the tip. Watch carefully. A braid hook length can often increase the number of bites.*
- *Never put barbel in a keep net.*
- *Before releasing it, hold the barbel upright against the flow of the river for as long as it takes for its strength to return. Once you begin to feel its muscles flex, you can let it go, safe in the knowledge that it won't turn belly up in the current.*

☀ SEASON – the basic season is June 16th to March 14th. The fishery opens at 7.30am and anglers must leave at sunset. The only exceptions are Bridge Pool and Parlour Pool where 11.00pm is the closing time.

🎣 TICKETS – there is a sliding scale of charges depending on the areas to be fished and the time of year. In essence, the cheapest day tickets cost around £8 per day, but these can escalate for the best areas at the best time of the year. For example, you have to book in advance for the Parlour Pool, but this holds three rods at a price of around £50. The best thing is to contact either the Fishery Manager on 01202 591111, the Head Bailiff on 01202 485262 or that legendary tackle shop, Davis Tackle, on 01202 485169 for more details. Remember that tickets must be booked and paid for in advance before you even set up a rod. Also, look very carefully at the rules on your ticket. These can be quite complex, but they do emphasise that no barbel must ever be kept in a keep net.

→ DIRECTIONS – the main entry to the Royalty is at Avon Buildings, which is just off Bargates in Christchurch. This is very close to the Christchurch by-pass. You will find Davis Tackle shop on the corner. There is a car park at the Avon Building. This is closed at dusk.

🛏 ACCOMMODATION – phone the Christchurch Tourist Information Centre on 01202 471780. Anglers speak highly of the Royalty View Guesthouse, 24 Fairfield, Christchurch, Dorset BH23 1QX – 01202 485362. Also recommended are the Grosvenor Lodge on 01202 499008 and the Royalty Inn on 01202 486310.

FISHING THE CHRISTCHURCH AREA

It's not just the Royalty that should attract your attention in this richest of angling areas. There's a lot more besides. In fact, for years, Christchurch has proved a holiday hotspot for coarse anglers and I've made my own pilgrimages there over the years. You can fish the Avon up river – the Winkton and Severals fisheries are particularly prolific.

And, on the Stour, the Avon's sister river, there is the fantastic Throop fishery. In fact, if push comes to shove, I'd almost say that I personally enjoy Throop as much as I do the Royalty. It's arguable that the fish aren't quite as big – but as the barbel run well into double figures, they're big enough for me! And there are lots of them. Moreover, they're just that tad less difficult to catch. Yes, the Throop is a must.

There are also some excellent stillwaters within easy driving distance, and my own favourite is Hatchet Pond. This is hardly a pond, but a lovely expanse of generally shallow water that holds a stunning head of fish – bream, carp and tench especially – set in beautiful surroundings.

There is even more. Why not try Christchurch harbour? This is a super place to fish and, aged ten, it's where I caught my first flounders – on tackle designed for roach, which I would have been pursuing had my parents not booked our annual holiday two weeks out of season! There's a lot more to Christchurch harbour. There are times when the bass come in numbers and the fishing with small spinners is absolutely absorbing.

There are also mullet – and a more rewarding but frustrating fish doesn't swim anywhere in the world. The water in front of you can be black with mullet and you will still not get a bite. At other times, you seem to be hooking one every cast. Try for them with normal roach-type tackle – four- or five-pound line, a float and a size ten hook with a small piece of bread flake as bait. Alternatively, try maggots or a very small redworm. Keep varying the bait until you find something that they like, but remember this preference can change from one day to the next. Fascinating fish in a marvellous part of the coarse angler's world.

SEASON – generally June 16th to March 14th.

TICKETS – permits for all the waters that I have discussed – along with good directions to the venues – can be obtained from Davis Tackle, on 01202 485169. If you are considering a stay of a week or more down in the area, why not try contacting Christchurch Angling Club at 4 Marley Close, New Milton, Hants BH25 5LL for membership? This excellently run club has miles of river on the Stour and Avon. Tickets for Hatchet Pond can also be purchased from the Forestry Commission, Queen's House, Lyndhurst SO43 7NH – 01703 283141. Also contact the Throop Fisheries on 01202 35532. Ringwood and District Anglers' Association also hold some tremendous day ticket venues – Northfield Lakes, for example, cover fifty acres of water. They also have High Town Lake on their ticket, which holds thirty-pound plus common carp. Contact Ringwood Tackle at 5 The Bridges, Ringwood or phone 01425 475155 regarding membership.

DIRECTIONS – ask when buying tickets for your chosen venue.

ACCOMMODATION – the Christchurch Tourist Information Centre on 01202 471780 can supply details of various kinds of accommodation in the area. There is also accommodation on the water at Throop. Apply to the Manager at South Lodge, Holdenhurst Village, Bournemouth, or phone 01202 35532. There is also camping at Hatchet Pond. Contact the Forestry Commission for details.

THE ISLE OF WIGHT

There is coarse fishing in and around this lovely holiday destination, though it's of the more modest kind and you're not going to rewrite the record books. Nonetheless, that shouldn't put you off: the Isle of Wight has a huge amount to offer for the family holiday and some attractive places to cast a float. There are all the usual species to be found on the island. Most waters hold carp, though a twenty-pounder really would be rated a major success. You'll generally find tench, roach and some bream. The Isle of Wight Freshwater Angling Association, 66 Merrie Gardens, Merrie Gardens Lake, Sandown, Isle of Wight, has plenty of water on its ticket, and a membership enquiry before heading out would be a good idea. The club owns water on the River Yar and some good lake fishing on Gunville Pond and Somerton Reservoir.

Moreton Farm, Bradin offers some top rate coarse fishing on a very prolific, even if small, pool – phone 01983 406132. There s some tremendous fishing for juniors at Jolliffes Farm, Witwell – phone 01983 730783. Gillees Pond has built up something of a reputation, and day tickets cost £2 from Scotties Tackle Shop, 11 Lugley Street, Newport, or 22 Fitzroy Street, Sandown. Don t neglect Bembridge harbour – the bass and mullet fishing can be excellent during the height of summer. Try and get down there either early or late, and make note of the tides as mullet like to come in on the flow.

TICKETS – in general, coarse fishing on the Isle of Wight is very reasonably priced, and all the tackle shops are helpful.

ACCOMMODATION – The Isle of Wight Tourist Board has huge amounts of information on accommodation and will help with fishery details. Phone them on 01983 813818.

❧ FEEDING THE SWIM ❧

Feeding a swim with either ground bait or lose feed is one of the big problems of most coarse fishing scenarios.

• *Do you feed heavily and run the risk of over feeding, or do you feed light knowing you might not be able to hold the fish? As a general rule, it's probably better to under- rather than over-feed. Keep the fish actively looking for bait.*

• *Little and often is generally better than a single mass bait attack. Be careful of putting ground bait over the heads of fish - especially bream - in very shallow water, especially in big balls.*

• *Be careful of putting out too much cereal ground bait during the summer. If it is not eaten it can simply lie and rot on the bottom, souring the swim for days.*

• *As a general rule, feed less in winter, in clear, cold conditions, and more in summer when the water is warm and coloured.*

• *If your swim suddenly goes off, it might not be your feeding that's to blame. A hungry pike may have been attracted by the activity of the show in front of you.*

• *If at all possible, try to buy the large catering cans of sweetcorn. These work out much more economical than smaller tins.*

• *In cold weather, enlarge the holes of a swim feeder with scissors or a shop bought hole enlarger, which will allow sluggish maggots to escape faster.*

• *Before ground baiting in the still water, throw in a little floating bread to check the amount of drift. In even a light wind, enough current can be generated to carry wrongly-positioned ground bait right out of the swim.*

• *When you are catapulting ground bait out, go for a low flow flight path in a wind, as it is less likely to be blown off course.*

BROADLANDS LAKE – HAMPSHIRE

The Broadlands Estate has long been a dream for game fishermen, as it straddles the River Test. There are very good chub in this stretch of the river but, sadly for us, it's reserved for the trout and salmon anglers. However, coarse fishing isn't forgotten and there's a glorious lake of almost three acres set in the grounds that offers some tremendous fishing. It's a beautiful water in a very special place and deserves mention.

Fish stocks are immense. For the general angler you can't do better than try the method feeder with maggot on the hook. Failing that, go on the waggler with four-pound line straight through to the hook – about right for the sort of fish that you're likely to hook. Okay, you'll come across a lot of bream in the skimmer class, but almost certainly as the day progresses you'll get better fish of four, five or six pounds. And doubles are always possible. The tench, too, feed well right into the autumn, and then, of course, there are the carp. There's a good head of twenty-pounders in the lake, with many fish in low and mid doubles, but it's the huge numbers of fish in the five- to nine-pound category that provide tremendous sport for the general angler. When that float goes down, you don't know if you're hooking into a two-pound skimmer, a double-figure slab, a five-pound tench or an eleven-pound carp – very appealing fishing.

There's also a stretch of shallow canal alongside the lake that is full of big fish. It's generally a pole and match water, but you can attack it successfully with a waggler.

SEASON – this runs from 1st March to 7th January.

TICKETS – these cost £7 a day and are available from tackle shops in Southampton but it is best to phone the tremendously helpful fishery manager, John Dennis on 07973 523358 to book your ticket in advance. This must be done. John will also advise you on the best way into the estate when he sends you your ticket. He is a fund of information and very welcoming indeed. Do note that there are only twenty-five pegs and these fill up quickly, so do book well in advance. Also, on some Sundays clubs book the whole lake for matches.

DIRECTIONS – pick up the A36 from junction 2 of the M27. At the first roundabout, take the A3090 north, and Broadlands is on your right shortly before you reach Romsey.

ACCOMMODATION – the Tourist Information Centres in Southampton, on 023 8022 1106, and Winchester, on 01962 840500, can give advice on suitable accommodation in the area.

KENNET AND AVON CANAL – BERKSHIRE

Very different from the river itself, the Kennet and Avon canal still provides some great fishing, especially in the Hungerford area where the Hungerford Angling club controls two tremendous miles. It's the sort of water that appeals to all types of anglers – specimen hunters flock for the big carp that run to over twenty pounds but there are lots of small bream, good roach and very good perch to keep the average angler happy.

29

Canal carp can be a bit of a conundrum, and my own fish have only come after intensive stalking operations. You'll often find them hanging very close to cover, so do look under bushes, reed beds or moored boats. Again, my own successes have tended to come in the winter, when they're moving very slowly indeed. If you can locate a group of fish and feed very gently and tightly, you'll probably get one or two of them going down during the course of the day – especially in the later afternoon. Casters are good, but also try dyed and flavoured sweetcorn and small redworms.

As for perch on canals, try and get a lot of small fish feeding with light ground bait and a sprinkling of maggots and you'll draw the predators in. Then a small dead bait or lobworm will often be picked up.

☀ SEASON – the basic season is June 16th to March 14th.

✦ TICKETS – these are available in advance from Howard's Pet Shop, Hungerford, on 01488 685314, or Field and Stream, Newbury, on 01635 43186. Day tickets are £3.

➡ DIRECTIONS – pick up the A338 from junction 14 of the M4. Head towards Hungerford. Once you reach the mini-roundabout, follow the sign for the town centre and pass under the railway bridge. Turn immediately right into Church Street and you'll find the canal.

▭ ACCOMMODATION – phone the Tourist Information Centre in Newbury on 01635 30267. They will be able to supply details of accommodation available in the area.

THE RIVER KENNET

The River Kennet must appear in any discussion on fishing in the south. The problem for the coarse angler is that it is very difficult to gain access to most stretches. It's a crying shame, but this is a lovely river and it's not surprising that clubs and syndicates have jumped in to claim the best of the water. However, there are one or two opportunities, and the fishing can be a delight.

One of my own personal favourites is Aldermaston Mill in Berkshire, which I've visited several times, seen endless amounts of barbel, and have yet to have anything like a red letter day. Mind you, I realise that's my fault rather than any slur on the river. The key to the Kennet is to fish as differently as possible. If everyone is using ledgered meat, then try free-lining a tiny scrap of pepperami. Only one example, I know, and one that might not work, but I hope you get my point.

It's quite traditional to fish a stick float and caster over hemp close in to snags. This method certainly does hook a lot of fish, but you can have problems getting them out – especially with barbel over six pounds in weight. It's far better, I believe, to bait moderately lavishly close to a known barbel-holding snag and then simply wait. Always resist the temptation to fish at once, but let the barbel build up their confidence. Beware of putting bait in once they're out feeding – this can unsettle them. If you are going to introduce bait, do it well upstream, so that the splash doesn't scare them, and let it drift down to them.

 SEASON – open 16th June to 14th March.

 TICKETS – from the Old Mill, Aldermaston, RG7 4LB on 01189 712365. Day tickets cost around £8 and directions will be given. It's also worth a quick enquiry to the Wasing Estate to see if any season tickets are still available there. This is a tightly run, beautiful little syndicate and worth taking seriously if you really want to fish the area. Mind you, tickets are like gold dust but try phoning on 01189 714281. Also contact Tony Jenkinson on 01737 643821 regarding day tickets for the river at Bull's Lock and also Calpac associate membership, a steal at £32 and one that opens a whole new window on the river.

 ACCOMMODATION – the Reading Tourist Information Centre, on 01189 566226, can advise on various types of accommodation in the area.

THE RIVER THAMES

Naturally enough, it's very difficult to pigeonhole the Thames into any one section of this book, simply because it passes through different counties on its way to the sea. However, the tidal Thames is a very different beast indeed, and away from the capital you've got some beautiful and very under-used fishing to explore. Mind you, exploration is very much the name of the game with much of the Thames.

The Thames is certainly a river with history. For centuries, it's been a major part of our angling heritage and has constantly made the headlines. Big barbel catches in the 19th century. A.E.Hobbs, the brown trout maestro of the early 20th century. Peter Stone's mammoth bream catches in the Oxford area in the 1950s. Strange then that the Thames should have drifted out of popularity for so long.

It's impossible in a book of this size to give a detailed introduction to the Thames – there's just too much of it, with too many permit holders, to make any sense whatsoever, so I'm going to concentrate on two of the most exciting lines of attack.

The first one is to contact Roger Wyndham Barnes, a professional guide on the river who concentrates on the stretch between Reading and Marlow. He's a perfect companion for the day and there is nothing he doesn't know about old Father Thames. A day out with Roger really is a wonderful experience. You'll probably be afloat in his large, comfortable boat, which is generally moored at the Compleat Angler Inn on Marlow weir. Roger will take you for whatever species you want, either in the weirs, on the main river or down in the backwaters. You could spend months, if not years, learning for yourself what Roger will teach you in a single day. Go on, treat yourself.

The other exciting way to tackle the Thames is to buy a permit for the locks and weirs on the river. The Environment Agency sells permits to eighteen Thames sites, including Buscot, Radcot, Sandford, Benson, Bell Weir and so on down the river.

The weirs are marvellous, thrilling places to fish. It's exciting just to get the key and be able to push through the gates marked 'Private'. You truly enter another world on a Thames weir pool.

You'll find virtually every fish swimming in British waters available to you. Barbel, chub, pike, roach, tench, bream, brown trout — you name it, the weir pools have it. Mind you, weir pool fishing isn't always easy. You've got to be able to read the water and fish the muscular currents effectively to get the best out of the experience. Once again, Polaroid glasses are essential: there will be times when you'll see fish in the shallower water and you can work out a plan of attack. Don't be afraid to be bold: big free-lined baits work well. Try two lobworms on a size six hook with perhaps a single SSG shot six inches up the line. Keep close contact with the bait as it trundles along the bottom, and don't allow slack to develop or you could miss that crucial tug.

Try stret-pegging. Sit upstream of the main flow and use a float set three or four feet over depth. In effect, you're ledgering, but the float allows you to lift the weight up every few seconds and let it resettle. It also gives you perfect bite indication and allows you to know exactly where your bait is working.

We're not just talking barbel and chub in this quick water: most of the weir pools have slack areas and here you can find tremendous tench working in the weeds. Early morning is the best time to be out for the tench, and most other species in fact, and that fresh period of the day only enhances the extraordinary beauty of the experience.

If you do take out a weir pool ticket I'm sure you will be inspired to explore more and more of the Thames, building up knowledge as you go. You'll meet river keepers who will give you tips and point you in the right direction. But the great thing about fishing the weirs is that you'll catch fish from the start, and that builds up confidence.

One of the joys of fishing the Thames is the total uncertainty of what you might catch next. Using a lobworm you could pick up a trout, a salmon, a barbel, a chub, a perch, a cracking roach, a huge dace, a tench, a bream, a carp, an eel, a flounder... I think you get the picture. And, what's more, there are some absolute crackers. The late, great Peter Stone caught most of his big fish from this river system and he always felt a thirty-pound river carp was just round the corner for him. Sadly, he didn't quite make it, but that was neither his fault nor this splendid river's. Piking from autumn through the winter can also be excellent.

SEASON – the Thames is currently under the blanket closed season of 14th March to 16th June, but this is under review.

TICKETS – contact Roger Wyndham Barnes at 4 Montreal Terrace, Twyford, Berks RG10 9ND or phone him on 01189 342981. The lock and weir fishing permit, available from the Environment Agency, must be applied for at least ten working days before required use. Write to the Environment Agency, PO Box 214, Reading, RG1 8HQ. Permits cost £21 for adults and £14 for seniors and juniors.

ACCOMMODATION – the Tourist Information Centre can supply details of accommodation in their area. Phone 01189 566226. Roger Wyndham Barnes will also advise on accommodation if you are spending the day with him.

Whether you're fishing a large water or a small commercial fishery, camouflage yourself, move with caution, and your catches will improve. It's an essential art form that is all too frequently overlooked.

A lovely, old-style lake carp, a fish stocked back in the 1950s that had grown slowly to an imposing size. Carp like this are now found in many of the commercial waters springing up around the country.

A pike caught on a sea dead bait. Bite indication is absolutely essential with this method. A float will show you exactly when a fish has taken the bait, and you should strike at once.

But you don't have to use dead baits. More and more anglers are beginning to discover the joys of fly fishing for pike. This particular fish was taken on a big artificial lure fished just under the surface.

Commercial waters offer tremendous fishing opportunities in safe, protected environments. Stocking policies are invariably generous and good sport can virtually be guaranteed.

The Fens are not everybody's cup of tea, but at sunset, these long, straight waters can have a beauty of their own, especially if you're a keen bream or predator angler!

GOLD VALLEY LAKES – HAMPSHIRE

These are really beautiful waters – very well managed, surrounded by trees and holding excellent fish stocks. They've become very popular pleasure and match venues over the years and hardly surprisingly: even in cold weather, big bags can be built up. There's pretty well everything here, but ask advice from the fishery manager, who will locate the water most suited to your needs. There are good carp, excellent roach and the crucian fishing can be fantastic.

The carp are the major draw at Gold Valley, and it pays to bait heavily for them. If you skimp on food, then your catch will suffer. Remember that carp, especially in commercial fisheries, can be very greedy fish, so take enough feed with you.

☀ SEASON – open all year.

🐟 TICKETS – day tickets cost £10 for one rod and £15 if you're doubling up for the carp. Book them in advance on 01252 336333.

➡ DIRECTIONS – take the M3. At junction 4, turn onto the A331, heading south. After two miles or so, turn left towards the station. It is also signed Mytchett. When you come to the junction with the A321, turn right. At the next pub, turn right again, go under a low bridge and cross the dual carriageway. You'll find the lake signposted 'Spring Lakes Country Club'.

🛏 ACCOMMODATION – details of various kinds of accommodation can be obtained from the Tourist Information Centre in Aldershot on 01252 320968.

❧ HIGHLY RECOMMENDED FISHERIES ☙

- *Longleat, Warminster, Wiltshire. Famous old water in the grounds of a beautiful stately home. Three stream-fed estate lakes hold carp to over thirty pounds, big bream, tench, perch, roach and rudd. A lovely fishery. Phone 01985 844496 for further details.*
- *Todber Manor, Todber, Dorset. Very popular match water. Big bags of carp possible on sweetcorn, maggot, caster and bread. Some quality crucians. Phone 01258 820384.*
- *Golden Pond, Stockbridge, Hampshire. Some excellent roach, good carp fishing and a few exotics – the crucian fantail crosses are particularly spectacular. For more details call 01264 860813.*
- *Hightown Lake, Ringwood, Hampshire. Mature twenty-two acre pit – big carp (over thirty pounds), big pike, bream and tench to seven pounds. Attractive water with some excellent fish. Tickets £7.50 a day. Phone 01425 471466.*

COARSE-FISHING SITES
IN THE SOUTH EAST

1. Rushmoor Lake
2. Bury Hill Fisheries
3. Tring Reservoirs
4. North Met Pit
5. Lake John Fishery
6. The River Lea
7. The Fennes Fishery
8. London's Parks
9. Wylands International Angling Centre

'A lot of the fishing hereabouts in the Greater London area might not be of the most attractive sort if it's just rolling valleys and mountains you're into, but believe me, John, there are some real whackers to be caught.'

MARTIN LOCKE, BAIT AND TACKLE SPECIALIST AND FAMOUS CARP ANGLER

A nd Martin was right. I suppose in the main he was talking about the great featureless gravel pits where people like him are quite willing to sit and wait a season out for a single run and to land the fish of their dreams. I haven't really included waters like this in this section – if these are the fish you want, you'll know exactly where to go yourself. Perhaps I haven't talked much about fifty-pound carp waters, but there's still a great deal that is of interest. You can catch barbel to double figures virtually within sight and sound of the M25. Or you can catch double-figure zander down in Surrey, along with huge pike. And how about the massive bream, roach and even catfish up at Tring? The Thames itself is on the way back and needs some investigation. Remember that huge stretches around the city can be fished for free and now hold endless number of species. So, all in all, the lot of the Londoner isn't that bad at all, and if you're here visiting, then you can have the best of both worlds: Europe's most dazzling city together with somewhere to cast a line, often only a tube journey away.

Many of the waters in the south-eastern area are comparatively crowded and noisy, but not all of them by any means. Some of my very best stations ever were spent on Tring Reservoirs – Wilston in particular. These were magical times, and camping in the woods was a true delight. The bream weren't always obliging, but when they moved in, the excitement was intense. Big fish rolling, breaking the water under the moonlight – the bobbins never still as the line is continually brushed by the big, bronzed bodies. And then, a bite... the bobbin screeching to the rod butt, the reel beginning to backwind. A strike. An enormous resistance and then a blow on the rod tip as though a bag of cement has buried it. Great days indeed, in a fabulous setting.

THE SOUTH-EAST

RUSHMOOR LAKE – SURREY

Rushmoor Lake is a beautiful water and absolutely ideal for beginners – the sort of place the family can have a very happy day out. It's a small water of around an acre, generally shallow, but dipping in places down to seven or eight feet. It's set in attractive countryside and the bird life is tremendous. It's mature, well established and it really gives you the feeling of being away from the town. The car park is close by, so you can set out the picnic things as well.

There are carp and bream running to six or eight pounds or so, but most of the fish present are just a few ounces up to a pound. These include tench, chub and crucian carp. There are also golden orfe, koi and all manner of exotics – the sort of species that really bring smiles to young faces. And because there are plenty of fish, the water is clouded and the fishing isn't too difficult. Big fish aren't the order of the day here, so you won't find the bivvies and the bite indicators that mar so many other waters. No, this is a friendly, well-looked-after little water that's ideal for the beginner.

All baits work well, but probably casters and maggots are as good as anything to build up a good mixed bag. Fish them under a float, and remember that no keep nets are allowed and you can only use barbless hooks – two ideal rules for novices.

☀ SEASON – open all year round.

✦ TICKETS – only eight day tickets per day are issued on this small water and they must be bought in advance at the Post Office in Rushmore itself. Contact Dennis Smaile on 01252 793698. The nearby tackle shop, Greyshot Tackle, can also give advice on 01428 606122.

➝ DIRECTIONS – from the A31, turn right at Hindhead traffic lights. After some quarter of a mile, turn right and look for the Pride of Valley pub, which is on the left. The entrance to the lake is about a quarter of a mile past the pub on the right.

⊨ ACCOMMODATION – the Tourist Information Centre in Guildford, on 01483 444333, can advise on accommodation in the area.

BURY HILL FISHERIES – SURREY

Bury Hill has long been one of the really revered waters on the big fish circuit, and I remember years ago being in awe of the galaxy of famous anglers that trekked to its banks. Mind you, Bury Hill offers more than big fish alone: it's beautiful, it's friendly, there's plenty of advice on hand and there are fish galore. But let's look at everything in a little bit more detail.

In my early days, Bury Hill consisted of just one large, twelve-and-a-half-acre lake, the water that is now known as Old Bury Hill. This is still a magnificent water, and although it offers seventy or so pegs, there are still plenty of opportunities to get away from any semblance of a crowd. Try booking a punt and getting up into the Jungle– an overgrown area that's inaccessible from the bank. The tench and carp fishing there can be excellent, with big specimens of both species. Eight- and even nine-pound tench are not unknown! Try fishing close to obstructions – reeds, trailing branches and the like – with a float and corn or pellets. Mind you, you've got to use heavy gear because these fish are big, they fight well and the Jungle looks exactly as it sounds.

If you can't get up to the Jungle, don't despair. The Boathouse, which is the deepest part of the lake at around twelve feet, produces some tremendous bags of tench. I also like the Front Bank, where the bottom shallows to only a couple of feet or so. It's quite possible to stalk fish there, and there isn't a more exciting way of fishing.

Old Bury Hill fishes well from spring onwards. You've got everything to go at – bream to ten pounds, tench to nine pounds, crucians to five pounds, good roach, big rudd and perch that can top the three-pound mark. Just think – cast out a big juicy lobworm and you've got every chance of catching a specimen fish of at least six different species. Incredible. Mind you, Old Bury Hill does benefit from a careful approach. Look for your fish, think how you're going to fish and devise a good plan of attack. Why not bait up two patches so that you can look for fish moving in? Try an over-depth waggler and twitch it back along the bottom. Straight sweetcorn is a great bait, but try grains that are flavoured and coloured. Black is one of my own personal favourites. Try natural baits; any sort of worm can bring an instant bite.

From the autumn onwards, Old Bury Hill moves into its predator mode and there is some of the best zander fishing in the country to be found here. And the pike fishing isn't bad either! Stocks of both fish are extensive, and you can expect zander into double figures and pike over twenty pounds if you're lucky.

The zander themselves are a great challenge. Sometimes you can get steaming runs from them, but if there's the slightest hint of resistance, your bait will be dropped like a hot brick, so fish carefully, sensitively and intelligently. The Island is great for zander packs and you can't beat the Jungle for big, roaming pike. If you haven't caught anything throughout the day, don't pack up early because the last couple of hours are particularly good, especially for the zander. And if you're still struggling, try to get your small dead bait as close into the snags as possible – always bearing in mind that you've got a duty to pull the fish out! Don't go light for predators either. Twelve- or even fifteen-pound line is a must.

Ten years or so ago, another couple of lakes were constructed on the site – Bond's Lake and Milton Lake. Bond's is a popular match water, but it's also great for children as it's absolutely packed with smaller fish and it really is the place to get a good number of bites. The carp aren't huge – up to about ten pounds or so – but they fight well and they come along in great shoals.

Milton Lake is something a bit more special. It's got some really first-class crucian carp fishing. And crucians really are one of my own favourite summer species. They're just so enticing. How do you convert those bites into fish hit? It's possible to get a dozen crucian bites and not hook a single one. It's even possible not to know you've even had the bites in the first place. For that reason, set up a float rig as sensitively as you possibly can. It also makes sense to fish close in – especially under any sort of cover. Crucians are very much margin feeders but they don't like to expose themselves to the sun's rays. Bait up carefully for crucians. A little mashed hemp seed drives them crazy. Try a single pink maggot on the hook. A pinch of breadflake is also good.

Bury Hill gives you the whole package – car parks, shops, toilets, caf s, resident bailiffs and even fishing instruction. Highly recommended.

SEASON – Bury Hill is open all year round, apart from Christmas Day.

TICKETS – these are available from Bury Hill Fisheries, Estate Office, Old Bury Hill, Dorking, Surrey RH4 3JU, or phone 01306 88833621. Rods cost £9 for the day with juniors, senior citizens and disabled coming in at £5. There are also evening tickets available. Boats are attractively priced at £5 per person.

DIRECTIONS – Bury Hill Fisheries is just off the A25 Dorking to Guildford road. It is less than a mile from Dorking town centre. Leave the town and you will see the fishery clearly signed on the right. There's a brown tourist sign advertising it.

ACCOMMODATION – the Tourist Information Centre in Guildford, on 01483 444333, will be able to advise on accommodation in the area.

TRING RESERVOIRS

Over the past twenty years or so Tring Reservoirs – that is Wilstone, Startops and Marsworth – have built up a reputation as big fish waters. Indeed, during my time on them, it was big or bust – generally in those days, with limited techniques, tackle and baits, it was bust! Today, you'll still find a lot of long stay anglers who are pursuing the big bream, massive tench, elusive catfish and increasing numbers of carp. There are also very big roach, especially in Startops. These anglers are prepared to sit for virtually a season, fishing hard for potentially mind-blowing rewards.

However, the Tring system is often overlooked by the more casual anglers in favour of the smaller commercial fisheries. This is a great shame. All three reservoirs are very lovely – my own favourites being Wilstone and Marsworth. They're set in lovely countryside with quality fish. Moreover, on Startops especially, if you contact the roach and perch you will be catching fish of a pound or so in succession.

SEASON – open all year round.

TICKETS – contact Bernard Double, the excellent bailiff, on 01442 822379. Day tickets cost under £5 – very reasonable for the stamp of fishing available.

DIRECTIONS – the Tring group of reservoirs is found just north of Tring. Take the A41 west and in a couple of miles turn right onto the B489. The reservoirs will be in a mile or so on the right hand side. The car parks will be signposted.

ACCOMMODATION – the Tourist Information Centres in Aylesbury, on 01296 330559, and Hemel Hempstead, on 01442 234222, can advise on accommodation in the area.

NORTH MET PIT – HERTFORDSHIRE

I'm moving a bit off normal territory here to talk about a season ticket water as opposed to a water available to the casual angler. I'm making this exception because North Met Pit, a mature gravel pit controlled by Lee Valley Parks, really is well worth investigating. This whole area is a maze of water, set in unspoilt countryside close to the M25. It's a real jewel.

North Met Pit itself extends to virtually sixty acres and holds some very big fish. The carp can get to forty pounds and average in the mid-twenties. The bream reach double figures, and the tench aren't far behind. There are good perch and roach, too.

These big gravel pits take quite a bit of reading, and perhaps they're not waters for the out and out beginner. Most carp fall to traditional tactics – boilies, buzzers and so on. Bait quite heavily, because there are numbers of big fish in the water, but always be prepared to move if you're not getting action. Remember that carp on big waters such as this do tend to follow the wind and it's not unusual to see anglers, gear in wheelbarrows, on the move as the wind swings round in serious fashion.

North Met is an attractive water studded with islands, bays and bars with plateaux. It's a snaggy water too, and can be weedy in summer. In short, it's a water for the tactician, the man who's prepared to put in his research, do his homework and get things absolutely right.

As it's such a big carp venue, the bream, tench and roach tend to be overlooked somewhat, but sport can be really good on swim feeder maggots. Also expect the odd carp to come along as well, falling for a tactic that's different. There are plenty of tench in the water, so you're not really sticking your neck out. You can expect three or four fish a session comfortably, and some of these could well be big ones.

The big pit scene isn't for everyone and it does demand a certain level of expertise, but once you're into it, it's a difficult obsession to let go. The fish are big and they're generally in top condition. North Met Pit does offer a very attractive, comparatively accessible way into the big pit scene. The south east is studded with these waters – Yateley, Darenth and so on – and it's tempting to go in at the very top of the ladder. Don't. Go for a water that's attractive, has a big head of fish and isn't too difficult.

The problem is that if you go for one of the very difficult waters it's not at all unusual to have an entire season there without a single fish to your credit. Even a bite is seen as a triumph. Save this type of ordeal for later.

SEASON – open all year round.

TICKETS – North Met Pit, Cheshunt, Hertfordshire, on 01992 709962. Tickets cost from £75 a season downwards, according to number of rods and concessions.

DIRECTIONS – take the A10 towards Cheshunt. Turn off into Cheshunt and join the B176. Heading towards the station, access can either be through Windmill Lane or Cadmoor Lane. You'll also find car parks accessible from the B194 at Fishers Green.

ACCOMMODATION – call Hertford Tourist Information Centre on 01992 584322 for details.

LAKE JOHN FISHERY – ESSEX

This is another water just north of the M25, which is an absolute must for a fishing-mad youngster. In fact, there are two lakes available for fishing here. The lower lake is shallow, can accommodate about twenty anglers and is very heavily stocked. The water holds carp, tench, roach, rudd, bream, perch and chub. There are some good fish, too, with carp just into double figures, bream to five or six pounds, tench to three pounds and roach and rudd nudging the one pound mark. And they're all quality fish, too. One of the nice things about the fishery is that the manager, Colin Bartlett, is always round and about, offering

⚜ LONG DISTANCE FEEDER ⚜

When you're fishing reservoirs, big pits and large lakes, the long distance feeder is a really useful technique for bream, tench, roach and even carp.
- *Decide on what feeder you are going to use. If it's a closed feeder, you're probably going to be using maggots as both loose feed and hook baits. With an open feeder, you can mix a firm ground bait up and work in all sorts of particle baits such as casters and sweetcorn.*
- *A closed feeder is particularly good in the winter, in clear water when the fish are picky and you're not expecting many bites.*
- *A big, open feeder probably works better in the summer when the water is warm and you're expecting more activity. However, remember, there are no hard and fast rules in fishing.*
- *Decide on your bite indication. You can either use a quiver tip rod, a swing tip or some kind of butt indication. Quiver tipping is big at the moment but butt indication can work better if the fish are very finicky.*
- *If bites are not materialising properly, think about your hook length. Lengthening it – even to four or five feet – can work wonders.*
- *Be accurate with your casting. There is no point casting as far as you can each time if your direction is wayward. You won't build up a baited patch that way. Don't strive for distance until you have accuracy sorted out.*
- *Don't go too light on your main line. Remember that punching out a feeder all day long exerts great strain on your tackle.*
- *There are all manner of complicated feeder rigs in the press at the moment. Choose a simple one to begin with that isn't too complicated to tie up. Don't make life more complex than it needs to be.*
- *Don't keep fish in keep nets unless you really have to, for example, fishing a match. This is especially important in the summer when oxygen levels are low.*

advice and just keeping his eye on the children's safety. This gives the place a friendly feel and makes it an ideal starting ground for kids. Mind you, it isn't too bad for Mum or Dad either!

The top lake is somewhat deeper, going down to around ten feet. Every day, good catches of carp and tench are put together, especially if you fish neatly and tightly, perhaps under a float with sweetcorn or small cubes of meat. Maggots also work well, but the fish aren't stupid and you've got to approach them carefully. The top lake also produces the odd big fish, and you'll see twenty pounders cruising and occasionally caught. All in all, a really well thought out and worthwhile little fishery that offers a great deal of scope for the angler who is climbing the fishing ladder.

☀ SEASON – open all year round.

✦ TICKETS – these cost £4 for half a day and £6 for a full day. Call Colin Bartlett on 0958 938153. Barbed hooks are not allowed and keep nets can only be used in matches (and then they have to be disinfected first). Another nice touch is that boilies too are banned.

➜ DIRECTIONS – from Waltham Abbey, take the A121 eastwards as far as the Crooked Mile roundabout. Take the second exit towards Upshire. Turn left into Galley Hill Road and continue for a mile until you reach Aimes Green. Turn left and follow the road to the fishery.

⊨ ACCOMMODATION – contact the Tourist Information Centre in Waltham Abbey, on 01992 652295, who can supply details of accommodation in the area.

THE RIVER LEA

This, of course, is the famous river of Isaak Walton's *Compleat Angler* and even today, hundreds of years down the line, it has some very interesting fishing on offer. The Lea flows through Bedfordshire and Hertfordshire and then along the boundary between Essex and Middlesex before it joins the Thames. It's forty-six miles long and urbanization and the creation of canals have destroyed a great deal of what Walton would have recognised back in the 17th century. Nevertheless, the river still holds good carp, bream and roach – especially where there are canals – and very impressive barbel and chub in those stretches that are still freely flowing. Whilst there are barbel now well up in Hertfordshire, it's probably King's Weir Fishery that most people have heard of and this is the most famous piece of the river today. The fishery combines both the pool and a good few hundred yards down river. It's a cracking place, and even if it's not quite what it once was, you still have to book in advance.

The king of the Lea is Fred Crouch, a true gentleman and an excellent barbel fisherman. It's his opinion that the pool won't produce the same bags as it did in the past, but it's still an inspiring place to fish. Fred's tips are to put in a good amount of loose feed with either a feeder or a bait dropper and, as he says, 'Invite them out of the snags to feed'. Fred's favourite baits for the Lea are maggots, hemp and luncheon meat, but chopped into very tiny cubes indeed so the fish aren't alarmed. After baiting up, Fred likes to leave the swim for an hour, if not two, so the barbel really do move onto the feed and become confident. The problem with fishing immediately is that if they even feel the line, they'll be off, running for sanctuary. So don't rush things. Also don't neglect getting your bait very close in to the side. Remember that barbel love to have the bank at their backs.

A good example of the other side of the Lea is at Enfield Lock in Middlesex. Like much of the river, this lock section is now run by the Lea Angler's Consortium, who have initiated a major stocking programme in recent years. Carp arc now the main culprits but big tench are present. The marshes north of the lock are famed for tench, bream, chub and some of the bigger carp. South of the lock, behind the Riffles pub, there are pike – some of them good ones. Pole fishing off the high wall in front of the pub is also popular for perch, roach and so on. Overall, sweetcorn, maggots, worms, hemp, boilies and humble breadflake are the baits that work here.

Two venues on the Lea to tempt you. If the river grabs your affections – and there's no reason why it shouldn't – then you'll want to begin exploring and finding new stretches. Much of it is private but a good deal is available on day ticket.

SEASON – as I write, the closed season on rivers still remains 14th March to 16th June. This writer hopes the closed season is maintained.

TICKETS – for King's Weir Fishery phone 01992 468394 to book day tickets in advance. These are £7 and rules include no wading, no boilies or live baits. It's also compulsory to have unhooking mats with you and remember no barbel – or any species come to that – can be put into keep nets. Day tickets at Enfield Lock cost £3. Call 01279 654434 for details.

DIRECTIONS – King's Weir is situated at Wormley, just north of Waltham Cross. To find Enfield Lock, turn off the A10 into Ordinance Road. Follow this past the level crossing to the main lights and go past the pub. Parking is available on the street next to the canal.

ACCOMMODATION – the Tourist Information Centre in Waltham Abbey, on 01992 652295, hold details of accommodation in the area.

THE FENNES FISHERY – ESSEX

The Fennes is one of the largest coarse fishing complexes in Essex and offers nearly fifteen acres of water, split between three spring-fed lakes. It's an attractive place to fish and the waters were originally excavated from flood meadows and now bear the name of the fields that preceeded them. It's a well thought out fishing complex. There's a shop, caf , good car parking and plenty of really sound advice so there's no need whatsoever to feel left out in the cold here. There's one thing about commercial fisheries – they need satisfied customers to succeed and at Fennes you get all the help you and your family, want. But let's look at the lakes.

At around six acres, Ash Grounds is probably the largest lake, and it's also the oldest. It's heavily stocked with all species of carp including ghosts and crucians. And what fish they are. You'll find some really tremendous individual specimens, testimony to the fishery's advanced stocking policy. There are good stocks also of tench, bream, roach and a few rudd. The average carp here aren't that large – fish of around ten pounds are to be expected. The bream run up to nine pounds though, and the best perch is just a shade under four pounds.

❖ CARP ❖

The South East really is the carp man's Mecca. The proliferation of gravel pit fisheries appearing over the last thirty or forty years has meant that there is an endless number of venues now available, and many of the fish in them are very big. Thirty-pounders are now relatively commonplace, whilst forties and even fifties are no longer the stuff of dreams. Mind you, this isn't easy fishing.

• *Read all you can about carp fishing before starting out. There's an extensive literature, so select the right book for your present level.*

• *Try to get as much information on your chosen water as possible. This is not always easy, but you will find some anglers and tackle dealers willing to help.*

• *Don't spend too much money on gear until you're quite sure you like the sport.*

• *Don't go in for very long stay sessions until you're more experienced. Your first days at the waterside ought to be measured in hours rather than days or weeks.*

• *You'll probably start off by using a bolt-rigged boily setup. It makes sense to buy shop-bought baits at first. Don't complicate your fishing by making your own. It's wise to start at a smaller commercial fishery where there are plenty of medium-sized fish. This way, you gain experience of carp behaviour and how they fight. Don't begin at the top rung of the ladder. Chances are you won't get a bite, and if you do hook a fish, it will be too big and powerful for your experience.*

• *Even though I don't recommend very expensive tackle to begin with, you have a duty to the fish to make sure it is sound and won't let you down in a fight.*

• *Remember that once you've landed a carp you really do have to look after it, in part because it is a very expensive item for the fishery owner. Always lay it on an unhooking mat and get it back in the water as quickly as you possibly can, perhaps after an admiring glance and a quick photograph.*

• *Join the Carp Society (01367 253959) and go to their regional meetings. Here you'll find like-minded carp fanatics who are willing to pass on advice.*

• *Don't be intimidated. The carp world initially seems one riddled with secrets and superstars. Take your time and the knowledge will begin to come.*

Ash Grounds is a natural water with islands and plenty of marginal reeds, including reed mace, bulrushes and water lilies. Obviously, all this shelter gives the angler a lot of target areas where he can either use a pole or a running line. But, as ever, make sure that your tackle is up to the job.

All normal baits work – sweetcorn, luncheon meat and maggots – and don't overlook floating baits for the carp. As winter pulls in, most of the fish tend to migrate towards the deeper water close to the car park but it's always worth walking the lake, even in the depths of winter, to see what's working in the shallows.

Hobb's Croft Lake is between three and four acres in extent and has a cracking head of carp, several running to just over the twenty pound mark. There are good heads of bream and tench also approaching seven pounds and, once again, there are good crucians, roach and perch. Most of the lake is shallow – about three feet or so – but there is a deeper section where the depth plummets to eight. This shallow water means that float fishing is generally the favoured line of attack.

Hill and Black Lake is a little way from the main complex and isn't always available, as it's hired out for matches. Mind you, when it isn't, try and get on there, because there really is a very big head of good fish in the water. Particularly interesting are the tench. They grow big and they're very powerful. Never neglect surface fishing in the summer here – it's a brilliant top-bait water.

SEASON – the Fennes is open from 7.30am until sunset, all year round with the exception of Christmas Day and Boxing Day.

TICKETS – apply to the Fennes Fisheries, Fennes Road, Bocking, Braintree, Essex CM7 5LB, on 01376 323285. Day tickets are £6 for adults and £4 for juniors. Evening tickets are available.

DIRECTIONS – heading towards Sudbury along the A131 from Braintree, turn off into Bocking Church Street, you will be directed by the brown Tourist Board signs. The fishery is then signposted half a mile down Fennes Road, which is a right turn by the village hall. Once again, you will see the brown Tourist Board signs. The car park and the two main lakes are on the left four hundred yards down a concrete road.

ACCOMMODATION – contact the Tourist Information Centre in Braintree, on 01376 550066. They can supply details of various kinds of accommodation in the area.

LONDON'S PARKS

There can't be a capital city in the world offering as many park and common pools as London. We tend to overlook how many green spaces there are within the M25 belt, and most of these have fishing available of one sort or another. For example, there are Pen Ponds in Richmond Park, Perch Pond and Hollow Ponds, the Ornamental Water and the Wake Valley Pond all in Epping Forest. We've got the Leg of Mutton Pond, the Rick Pond, Diana Pond, Heron Pond and the Long water all in the Royal Parks. There are the free ponds on commons such as Clapham and Tooting, for example, and that's just scraping the surface.

Of course, not all of the ponds offer top-rate fishing but you'd be surprised at the varieties and quality of the fish available. However, you've got to remember that these are very public places and there are periods when it is wise to avoid them. For example, a Bank Holiday Monday is not the best time to be on one of the commons. Night fishing might sound the ideal option but I've had my own scares on the commons in the past and would certainly advise against it – even in permitted places. At the very least, go with a couple of friends.

If I have to give one time when it's best to be out on these waters it must be the very early morning – preferably when the dew is still about. This is when you'll see the London parks and commons at their best anyway and you'll be amazed at the amount of wildlife tripping past, or leaving signs in the dew. This is when the fish are feeding at their best. Even though most of these are not particularly big waters, do take the time to walk round them and don't rush into settling on a swim. If possible, look for feeding fish. Sweetcorn is a good general bait and so too are maggots. Take a loaf with you perhaps, and scatter a few pieces of crust in the margins and you'll be surprised at what will come up: I once had a one-and-three-quarter-pound crucian from Clapham Common on a floating dog biscuit!

The size of that crucian carp shouldn't come as a surprise: there are some pretty hefty fish in these park lakes, far bigger than one would expect. Perch, at least until relatively recently, could grow large, and there are some very big tench about. Even if you don't see carp, that doesn't mean to say that they're not present. It's more likely that they've learned to lie low. There are occasional stray big pike too, and I have an inkling that you could be in for a surprise if you tried a bit of eel fishing. All in all, these are very handy waters and there are some that should be taken seriously.

SEASON – the contact numbers will advise.

TICKETS – for Pen Pond, contact the Park Superintendent on 020 8948 3209. For Perch Pond, Hollow Ponds, the Ornamental Pond and Wake Valley Pond, contact the Superintendent on 020 8532 1010. For the other ponds in the Royal Parks, contact the Garden and Estate Manager on 020 8781 9610.

WYLANDS INTERNATIONAL ANGLING CENTRE – EAST SUSSEX

Wylands is a super place, either for the individual angler or the whole family. There are well over a hundred and fifty acres of rural countryside to be enjoyed – water, woodland and pasture. There are specialist carp lakes and general waters where you can just about catch anything that swims. There's also the county's largest single match lake, which again heaves with fish. Wylands really is proof that a commercial fishery can settle naturally into the landscape and be of huge benefit to both fishermen and wildlife in general. It's a perfect holiday destination – there's on-site accommodation in self-catering chalets, touring caravans and there's a campsite available if you want to bring your own tent. The snack bar is well stocked and the woodland walks are a treat.

The new Specimen Lake is only about two acres in size but there's a large island and a natural feel to the place. Carp reach well into the twenty pound mark and there are some big rudd and tench. Kell Lake and House Lake also hold big carp. In fact, there are a total of five lakes in the complex where twenty pounders can be anticipated.

Field Lake is an absolute beauty, only about an acre in size but heavily stocked with small carp and tench – fish averaging between one and three pounds. Exactly the sort of place to bring on a budding juvenile angler or two while father or mother enjoy themselves hugely. And if you want to get very traditional, there's Roses Lakes. There are no carp in here and therefore none of the internal bleeping of optonics that you come to expect on so many waters. In fact, only pole, float and feeder fishing are allowed for the extensive stocks of tench, roach and rudd. A lovely little place – new but settled nicely into the landscape.

These commercial fisheries, as I've said before, really fill a niche and it would be a mistake to think of them as being too easy. These are waters that allow you to enter at any level. Kell Lake, in particular, really does set a challenge to even a skilled carp angler. On the other hand, if you've barely held a rod in your hand before, you're still going to get bites and action.

☼ SEASON – open all year round, twenty-four hours a day.

⚔ TICKETS – contact Wylands International Angling Centre, Powdermill Lane, Catsfield, Nr. Battle, East Sussex TN33 0SU, on 01424 893394. Day tickets vary but are on average between £6 and £7 per day with concessions for juniors.

→ DIRECTIONS – from Battle take the A271 westwards. Two or three miles from the town turn left onto the B2204 to Catsfield. In Catsfield, turn into Powdermill Lane and pass the Burntwood Hotel. Fifty yards further on you come to an open field with a wooden fence. At the end of the field turn into Wylands Farm Drive. It is well signposted.

⊨ ACCOMMODATION – you cannot do better, when fishing, than to live on site, and the chalets at Wylands are excellent. Phone for details. Alternatively phone the Tourist Information Centre in Battle on 01424 773721 for details of other accommodation in the area.

- *Wylands Farm, Battle, Sussex. Four specialist carp lakes and four multi-species lakes – ideal for novice and experienced angler alike. Carp to over twenty pounds, good tench, roach, rudd and bream. Also crucians. Contact Colin Bouner on 01424 893394.*
- *Northlands Park, Felmores, Essex. There are two main lakes here incorporating a conservation area. Plenty of bream in the two- to five-pound bracket. Quiver tip with sweetcorn. Good carp to twenty pounds, roach, tench and big perch. Also some big pike. Tickets £3. Contact Mick Toomer on 01268 282317.*
- *Birds Green Lakes, Fyfield, Essex. A four lake complex beside the river Roding. Good carp fishing, bream to eight pounds and some big tench. One lake holds large carp to thirty pounds plus. Something for everybody. Contact Philip Gadd on 01277 899645.*
- *Jacks Lake, New Barnet, Hertfordshire. Carp to twenty pounds taken on boilies and floaters. Pole fishing for roach, tench, skimmers and crucians. Day tickets £4. Contact Mick Hanley on 020 8364 8009 for further details.*

Coarse-Fishing Sites
in East Anglia

1. Earith Lakes
2. Northey Park
3. The Fens
4. Glen Mere Lakes
5. Bure Valley Lakes
6. Blickling Lake
7. Gunton Park Lake
8. Great Witchingham Lakes and River Wensum
9. Woodrising Water Meadows
10. Hickling Broad
11. Fritton Lake
12. Yew Tree Lakes
13. Alton Water
14. Ardleigh Reservoir

'You ask why I've moved down to Norfolk from Yorkshire, John? Well, here you've got the bloomin' lot. You've got so many different fish species and just look at the sizes they grow to. And some beautiful waters. I'm not saying I didn't have fun up north – and that's where I learnt my trade, I know – but there are few places to compete with what you've got down here in East Anglia.'

DAVE PLUMMER, AUTHOR AND HOLIDAY CONSULTANT, IN CONVERSATION WITH THE AUTHOR

And Dave was, of course, right. I first began to fish in East Anglia when I was a mere five years old and even then I realised how spectacular the fishing was. After all, what does the area not have? You can fish huge, reed-margined, serene broads. Or there are the rivers, some tidal, some fast flowing over chalk bottoms. You can investigate the growing number of gravel pits around the region. And every farm seems to have its own marl pit or pond. And then let's not forget the glory of the estate lakes. In North Norfolk , in particular, there is a string of impressive halls from the west to the east, and each one has its own carefully-sculptured lake. And if that's not enough, you can even take your pike gear, charter a boat from any one of a number of small ports and go a few miles off shore to fish for summer tope. Or, come to that, you can walk the shore line with a simple spinning outfit and catch yourself a bass or two.

And big fish abound. Over the years, the eastern counties have held the pike record, the rudd record, the bream record, and the zander record, and they've come close with both eels and roach.

East Anglia constantly springs surprises, even on those who have known it a lifetime. For example, in the centre of Norwich itself you can occasionally come across a big sea trout fresh up from the coast. Or how about the coastland marshes, frequently flooded but still capable of holding extraordinary tench, rudd, roach and pike?

Dave Plumber is definitely right. We do have the bloomin' lot!

EARITH LAKES – CAMBRIDGESHIRE

We are talking about a commercial fishery here, but one that has matured and holds good fish stocks. There are three lakes available, all on day tickets. They all hold good numbers of very nice carp. Mind you, Earith isn't simply a carp water. One of them, George's Water, although small, holds rudd approaching two pounds, and Pat's Pool, again small, holds tench well over seven pounds. The largest water, Pingree's Pool, holds good fish of many species, and there's even a rumour that there are decent perch about. These three small but charming waters are a delight to fish – there's a multitude of fish-holding features to look for, and bear in mind that the big tench will often cruise the margins. There's nothing more exciting than fishing a float under the rod tip and watching the bubbles fizz to the surface. Alternatively, try a very light feeder on one of the many gravel bars.

All the usual baits work here but tench, in particular, enjoy a little feast of casters. Switch to mini boilies, perhaps, and you also stand a chance of picking up one or two of the very fine carp. You'll enjoy Earith: there's a nice welcoming atmosphere, the surroundings are lovely and the fish really are in the best of condition. Perhaps that's something to do with the rules: you can only use barbless hooks; no carp or tench can be put in keep nets; you're expected to lay out an unhooking mat; and nuts are banned as baits – all good signs that the fishery is carefully watched over.

☀ SEASON – open all year.

✠ TICKETS – these are available on site at £6 with some concessions for Senior Citizens and juniors. Phone 01487 740701 for further details. Tickets need to be pre-booked.

➡ DIRECTIONS – from St. Ives, take the A1123 eastwards. You will shortly come to Earith village. Take the B1050 on the left. Take the second left and then the first left down the Earith Fen Drove. Car parking is on the left.

⊨ ACCOMMODATION – contact the Tourist Information Centre in Huntingdon on 01480 388588 for details of accommodation in the area.

NORTHEY PARK – PETERBOROUGH

Those that live around Peterborough sometimes lament about the quality of fishing, but with the opening of Northey Park – a three-lake complex – they've got something special now. These were originally gravel pits, but they've been left untouched for nearly thirty years and have matured magnificently. Today, they are reed-fringed and look as mature as any estate lake.

Rudd are the main species – a very overlooked fish in this day and age. The heavy stocking with carp in so many waters has tended to push rudd to the very fringes of existence in many areas. A tragedy, especially when you fish a place like Northey and see just what beautiful fish they are.

The rudd here, unfished for so long, are not particularly canny – yet! You can take them on a waggler outfit with corn, flake or maggots. There are some good fish and, although keep nets are allowed, do remember that rudd are fragile. My own advice is always to return them immediately after an admiring look. Feeder tactics will also work and why not drift out some floating bread and watch the shoals hammer into that. If you've got some casters that have gone off, let them float down with the breeze as well, and chances are that you'll see some cracking rudd come to the surface. In short, this is just the place to make you realise that the present day fixation with carp, barbel and pike is a blinkered one.

☀ **SEASON** – open all year round.
🐟 **TICKETS** – day tickets cost £5 on the bank. Contact 01733 558329 for further details.
➡ **DIRECTIONS** – Northey Park is situated on the Northey Road, Fengate, Peterborough, off the A1139, but it is advisable to contact the fishery for detailed directions.
🛏 **ACCOMMODATION** – try the Peterborough Tourist Information Centre on 01733 452336 for details of suitable accommodation.

THE FENS

To be quite honest, I've never personally really come to grips with the Fens, so I suppose I'm dubious about recommending them as a day-ticket venue to the more casual visitor. The endless drains and canals demand a specialist approach and are difficult to read. Location is always the problem, and in the deeper, more turgid waters there's rarely much visual sign to give you a clue. However, the rewards can be great. The bream and roach fishing can be sensational at times and, of course, predator action can shake the record books.

The Twenty Foot Drain, in Cambridgeshire, however, does buck the trend to some degree. Fish stocks are prolific and it does have some character, so if you do find yourself in this part of the country, it's well worth a look. As ever, location is something of a problem, but the Twenty Foot does have pointers. There is, for example, marginal weed growth, and you'll often find tench and bream very close in to the bank. Pole fishing is a favourite here. Look also for the bridges: historically hot spots and magnets to all fish species. Matches are frequently held along the length, so it pays to take a walk, talk to the competitors and see how they're fairing. And those that are doing well with silver fish could well give you a clue to the whereabouts of the zander and pike.

Feeder fishing is also a favourite: try casters, redworms or pink maggots on the hook. Don't expect bites to be tear-aways – look for slight nudges and concentrate like a hawk. And if you're new to the Fens, don't be alarmed if the flow suddenly speeds up – it simply means the pumps are in operation. Remember that you can be fishing something like a pond one moment and a roaring river the next. If it's any consolation, a change in flow can often mean a change in luck.

There are many who find Fenland fascinating. Perhaps to some eyes its unbounded flat acres appear bleak and uninviting, but you'll never see sunrises or sunsets anywhere else to compete. In fact, the skyscape is endless, only broken by occasional troops of poplars. It's an experience no angler should really miss.

SEASON – closed season March 14th to June 16th.

TICKETS – day tickets cost £3 on the bank. The fishing is controlled by Whittlesey AA, which can be contacted on 01733 203800. Please note that bloodworm is banned.

DIRECTIONS – from Whittlesey, take the A605 eastwards towards Wisbech. There are several roads leading off to the right that take you down to the water. Park close to the bridges or cross the drain and park even closer to your swim.

ACCOMMODATION – the Tourist Information Centre in Cambridge, on 01223 322640, will give advice on suitable accommodation in the area.

GLEN MERE LAKES – NORFOLK

I'm including this serene water simply because it's so very pleasant to visit and also because it's near to the north Norfolk coast, Cromer in particular, which is such an important holiday area. Glen Mere is a jewel. There are two lakes – one a syndicate water. They are both small, but with extraordinary stocks of fish.

Glen Mere is all about crucians – one of our most attractive, yet unsung, heroes. Here, they grow to about two pounds, but you will catch lots of fish beneath that weight. The fish fight well and also look stunning. All the more so when set against such a beautiful background.

There are carp – not particularly big ones – bream, roach and rudd, but none of them will make it into the record books. But does that matter? Fishing doesn't always have to be about earth-shattering experiences, especially if you can find a gorgeous little hideaway like Glen Mere.

SEASON – open all year round.

TICKETS – these cost £3.50 for adults and £2.50 for juniors. You pay on the bank. It's sometimes wise to contact the owner on 01263 761303 to check on availability.

DIRECTIONS – from Norwich, take the A140 north towards Cromer. At the roundabout before Aylsham, turn right and continue until you see the sign to Hanworth by the old stone cross. Turn left, cross one cattle grid and at the crossroads follow the sign to Sustead. Pass over the second cattle grid and after two hundred yards turn right into the fishery. You will see it signposted.

ACCOMMODATION – Cromer offers a wealth of bed and breakfast, guesthouse and hotel accommodation. Close by is the delightful country inn – the Saracens Head. Phone 01263 768909. The Tourist Information Centre in Cromer, on 01263 512497, can supply details of other accommodation in the area.

BURE VALLEY LAKES – NORTH NORFOLK

Bure Valley, situated in a wonderfully quiet, green part of North Norfolk, has splendid fishing. It consists of two lakes – one at a couple of acres and the larger one some four or five acres. The roach fishing in the smaller lake is superb and has been described as the best available on a day ticket anywhere in England. This small lake also holds good tench and plenty of carp.

The larger lake is a carp fisherman's paradise. The lake record is thirty-two pounds, but there are many fish over twenty pounds in weight, most of which can be seen cruising in the surface layers on warm days. As a bonus, pike fishing is soon to be allowed on a limited basis on the trout lake that is also situated within the fishery. It's confidently expected that twenty-, and even thirty-, pound pike will be caught there.

The big roach are generally caught on maggots or casters, float fished over a bed of ground bait or hemp. This doesn't mean to say that a lump of flake ledgered out in the middle might not pick up some fish. However, the water is usually clear, so a softly-softly approach generally works best.

Most carp fishermen approach the bigger lake using fairly standard tactics and bait, but success is to be had off the top with floating baits and fishing very close in around the margins, where there is a pronounced shelf. Particle baiting in these areas pays dividends for the careful angler. Above all, however, Bure Valley is an idyllic place to escape the pressures of the world and enjoy an entertaining conversation with fishery owner Mike Smith.

SEASON – open every day throughout the year.

TICKETS – carp lake £7.50 for twelve hours and two rods and £12.50 for twenty-four hours. The roach lake costs £5 for the day for two rods. There is no night fishing on it.

RECORDS – pike thirty-four pounds, roach two pounds twelve ounces, tench five pounds twelve ounces, carp thirty-two pounds eight ounces.

DIRECTIONS – Take the A140 from Norwich to Aylsham, then the B1354 to Saxthorpe. The fishery is on the right-hand side four miles out of Aylsham. You will find it down a mile long cart track.

ACCOMMODATION – The Buckinghamshire Arms on 01263 732133, The Saracen's Head on 01263 768909, or contact the Tourist Information Board on 01263 733903.

BLICKLING LAKE – NORFOLK

This great, crescent-shaped lake is the essence of an estate water. To the south lies Blickling Hall, one of the National Trust's prize mansions. The banks are heavily wooded. There are fields where sheep graze. To the north, beyond the dam, rolling countryside stretches to the coast. Blickling Lake, built over a chalky bottom, is fabulously rich and generally crystal clear unless clouded by swarms of daphnia.

This fertility is reflected in the fish stocks. Tench and bream are both numerous and very large. Double-figure bream and tench to eight pounds are always possible, along with excellent roach, big perch, massive pike and extraordinary eels. Carp, just a few ounces in weight, were stocked back in the mid 80s, and these have now grown into twenty- and thirty-pounders. Mind you, just because there are a lot of fish doesn't mean to say that Blickling is always easy. Far from it: the clear water and rich natural food stocks both make for fish that can be very picky. Yet, at the same time, to go too light is absolutely asking for trouble, especially from mid-summer onwards, when weed growth can be heavy.

So what do you do? Well, you can consider fishing at range from the dam, where the water is deep. A swim feeder with maggots or a small redworm on the hook often work well. Alternatively, patrol the margins with Polaroid glasses and actually look for feeding fish. You'll often find groups of tench browsing on the bottom, sending

❧ ESTATE LAKE TENCH ❧

Estate lake tench might not grow quite as big as some of their gravel pit brethren but, believe me, they are in marvellous condition, fight well and can be very difficult to outwit, especially in clear water.

The best times on most estate lakes are from dawn to about eleven in the morning.

• Try to visit the water before you are going to fish, to reconnoitre swims. If you can put some bait in beforehand, so much the better.

• Estate lake tench tend to be fairly territorial. You will find the same group of fish patrolling the same length of bank most days. If the water is clear enough, you can target groups of fish.

• If you're not getting bites, it's tempting to go light but remember these tench fight very hard and if there's weed about you will lose them.

• The top baits here tend to be maggots, casters, sweetcorn, lobworm, redworm and mini boilies.

• Float fishing is the traditional way to catch these fish but in very clear water they can be wary of both the float and the line in mid water.

• If you suspect that this is the case, it makes sense to ledger. Bolt-rigged tench baits are now very popular and bites do tend to be unmissable.

• Look for tench close to reed beds, especially bulrushes. Tench like to feed over relatively hard bottoms – sand, gravel and the like.

• To rake or not to rake! The traditional practice of raking a tench swim to stir up the bottom and excite their inquisitiveness has long been out of fashion, but my diving experiences suggest that a big cloud in the water does attract tench in.

up bubbles. Bait sparingly with casters, mini boilies or anything that doesn't cause too much commotion on entering the water. Bream seem to hang halfway up the lake, often rolling on the surface. Steady baiting up with a swim feeder can often get them down onto the bottom where they'll feed hard. This is how the big bags are amassed.

Top tench feeding times are from dawn till around ten or eleven o'clock in the morning. On a dull, windy day, you'll find the bream feeding well on into the early afternoon. Dusks can be productive but probably not quite as dynamic as the early morning period. The one problem can be a cold northerly that often blows in from the sea through the summer months, bringing with it a chilling mist. The whole lake can go quiet during these periods but once the winds swing round and the temperatures rise, look out for frantic feeding periods.

If you need any incentive to fish one of England's most beautiful lakes, be warned that the tench here fight probably better than anywhere else I know. Perhaps it's their general fitness or the clear water, but hooking one is like catching a tiger by the tail.

SEASON – open 16th June until March 14th, though for past few years has not closed until 31st March.

TICKETS – contact David Cooper, the park warden on 01263 734181 for details. £4 a day, £2 concessions. Tickets can be purchased on the bank.

DIRECTIONS – take the B1354 off the A140 from Norwich/Cromer road, which leads you through the town of Aylsham. Continue for approximately 1¼ miles to the north-west of Aylsham. Blickling Hall and lake is clearly signposted.

ACCOMMODATION – the Tourist Information Centres in Aylsham, on 01263 733903, or Cromer, on 01263 512497, can advise on suitable accommodation available in the area.

GUNTON PARK LAKE – NORTH NORFOLK

Gunton is a treasure of a water, some fifteen acres in extent, with depths varying between two and five feet. Created back in the 1700s as a feature for the grand house still standing today in the background, it is typical of the string of estate lakes to be found in this part of Norfolk. The lake and its surroundings are steeped in history: the car park is close to the ancient and unique water-driven sawmill, and you will almost certainly be fishing in view of the delightful two-century-old bridge that leads from the water up to the big house itself. In the north-east corner of the lake is an ancient, submerged boathouse.

Even the fish stocks are relatively ancient: the bream shoals, for which the water is justifiably famous, have been fished for decades. And there are scores of wild carp that escaped from a private lake deep in the estate and have flourished in the larger water. These wildies now often approach double figures, and you might even pick up the odd one going to twelve pounds or more. Thrilling stuff, especially if hooked on lighter bream gear. There are also roach, perch, pike, tench and a few crucian carp present.

Gunton Lake is fairly heavily fished, and most anglers use quiver tips, feeders and light hooks with maggots or caster as bait. This system works well, especially for the bream shoals that generally hang further out from the bank than the roach, carp or tench. However, it can pay to have a change: why not straight lead with a big lump of flake, for example? Or try a big worm over a bed of hemp and maggots. Hot areas include the eastern bank, the reed-bed bank and the north bank, but fish are also to be caught by the sawmill itself. My advice is not to put your basket down at the first free peg but have a good walk, watch the water closely, and you might see signs of feeding fish. This is where binoculars come in.

For the carp, try fishing close in amongst those reed beds. Particle baits of all sorts work well. But be warned – these fish aren't fools and you're going to have to present bait very tightly and delicately to trick them. My favourite would probably be a float-fished redworm over a carpet of hemp and casters.

SEASON – the old close season of March 14th to June 16th is roughly adhered to.

TICKETS – these are available on the bank and at present cost £3.50 per day for adults and £2 for children. The bailiff, the excellent Mr John Waite, will come round for the money.

RULES – please note that there is no night fishing and that boilies, keep nets and barbed hooks are also frowned upon!

RECORDS – bream run to eight or nine pounds, with rumours of ten-pounders. The wild carp generally plateau out at around eight to ten pounds but there is the odd mirror carp exceeding twenty pounds. Pike are rarely caught above twenty-two or twenty-three pounds. Roach average small but pounders are taken. The perch fishing is something of an unknown quantity, but big ones are present.

DIRECTIONS – turn right off the A140 from Norwich to Cromer about five miles north of Aylsham. The road to Gunton is called White Post Lane and is signposted Suffield. After a mile, you will see the gates of Gunton on a sharp right hand corner. Turn this corner and the fisherman's entrance is a hundred and fifty yards or so on the left. The lake is in front of you.

ACCOMMODATION – the Elderton Lodge, on 01263 833547, is situated on the estate itself and is personally highly recommended. The nearby Saracen's Head, on 01263 768909, offers excellent pub food and comfortable accommodation.

GREAT WITCHINGHAM LAKES AND RIVER WENSUM – NORFOLK

So much to say here I hardly know where to begin! Let's start with the Wensum, the scene of some of my own personal happiest fishing memories. But I'm going back a fair bit – to the 1970s to be exact. It was during that decade that I took hundreds – yes hundreds – of Wensum two-pound roach. There were also some threes thrown in and in fact I guess the Wensum was at that time probably one of the best roach rivers in history. Then came the bad times for all

This is the sort of carp that is now readily available in commercial fisheries. This beauty weighed well over twenty pounds and was taken from Bure Valley in Norfolk.

If you want to catch a pike like this one, which weighed just eight ounces shy of the forty-pound mark, then you'll have to head for a big Scottish loch, an Irish lough, the Norfolk Broads or perhaps a trout reservoir that allows occasional pike fishing. In case you are wondering, the blood on the

Crucian carp are stunningly beautiful and, thankfully, they are being stocked more and more in commercial fisheries. They are a fascinating fish, whose delicate bites can really infuriate.

pike belongs to the angler, not the fish! Cuts tend to bleed freely in the winter, so carry some antiseptic and a few plasters – and don't let the odd nip scare you off using sensible and safe unhooking techniques.

A wonderful roach, just under the two-pound mark, is every coarse fisher's dream. Such fish are still to be found in rivers, but some of the commercial stillwaters produce them in large numbers.

Look upstream of mills like this in the wintertime when roach and bream hunt out the deeper, slower water – their presence will also act as a magnet for pike.

manner of reasons – mainly, I guess, because of ill-advised river management – and the roach stocks declined almost to the point of extinction in many places. The good news? Well, little by little, it seems that pockets of roach are spreading and there are now fish to be caught.

In large part, this is due to changing attitudes. The Norfolk Anglers' Conservation Association has been at the forefront of this, and the Environment Agency also takes river management much more seriously and sensitively than it did before. So, there is hope for the future. A problem for the visiting angler is that most of the best stretches are not day ticket. However, there are still some opportunities. In Great Witchingham, about eight miles north of Norwich, there is a good stretch of water that holds a good head of chub and roach. It's controlled by the Great Witchingham Fuel Allotment Charity, who run both the river and the three lakes under their supervision with care.

How do you go about catching those fish? The chub are comparatively easy. I'd recommend roaming with a sensitive quiver tip, four-pound line and a loaf of bread. One or two swan shot, six inches from a size six hook should do the trick. Simply squeeze on some flake, cast it in all the likely spots – and there are many here – and if you don't get a response, move on. You could bait up a patch to come back to at dusk.

The roach can be more difficult. You will probably catch many chub to every single roach but, it could be that you might hit the jackpot. In fact, if you scale down the tactics I've mentioned above so you were using a size ten hook and a smaller piece of flake, you'll stand a chance of picking up both chub and roach. It's worth a try.

The lakes at Lenwade have been famous for at least forty years as this was a centre of extensive gravel workings just after the Second World War. Most are now, sadly, private but these three at Great Witchingham remain open to the public. They are beautiful lakes, and each offer something special. The lake on the right is primarily designed for carp and tench fishermen. It can get clear in the summer and is sometimes weedy, but you'll see fish gliding around. There are also a few, elusive very big crucians. The large lake to the left is an excellent bream water and the far lake – the long thin one – has good pike and some tench.

If you're really going to get after the bream, it's probable that you'll have to night fish. Put in a decent amount of bait – I don't recommend cereal – preferably on one of the bars. It pays, therefore, to get to the water early and do a fair bit of plumbing. Best baits include maggots, redworms and casters. If all else fails, try a good dollop of flake on a size eight. When a bream picks up your bait and runs, my advice is to have the reel on backwind and let the handle turn a few times before striking. It takes nerve to let a bite go on so far but you'll hit it in the end.

☀ SEASON – Open all year round.

🎣 TICKETS – these are available on the bankside. They cost £5 per day for adults and £1 for Senior Citizens and juniors. Night tickets cost £10 and £3 respectively. Please note that no carp are to be held in keep nets. Also obey the rule that says you must not drive up and

down the very bumpy track between dusk and 6.30am, for the sake of the nearby residents.
➡ DIRECTIONS – from Norwich, take the A1067 northwards towards Fakenham. You will
come into Lenwade (often called Great Witchingham) and cross the river bridge. Go past the
garage on your left and in quarter of a mile or so you will come to a butcher and a bakery.
Take the first left immediately after these shops and follow the bumpy track down to the waters.
🛏 ACCOMMODATION – the nearby Wensum Country Hotel (01603 872288) offers super
accommodation with its own fishing – both river and lake. Also apply to the Tourist
Information Centre in Norwich (01603 666071) for details of accommodation in the area.

WOODRISING WATER MEADOWS – NORFOLK

**If you're holidaying in Norwich and fancy a quick spin out, you can't do better
than visit this very attractive two-acre fishery. It's set well out in countryside
and surrounded by woods and meadows. It is man-made but you wouldn't
really know it: there are lots of features and nice depth changes. The fish stocks
are also excellent – good sized and very well-conditioned carp, tench and roach.
Pole fishing is a favourite here, but waggler and swim feeder also work well.
On a small water like this look for features – remember that tench hug the
margins of both the bankside proper and the islands. There's deeper water
away from the car park and fish tend to migrate down there as autumn turns
into winter. Get to the water early, however, and you can see a lot of action up in
the shallows near the car park.**

There are times when small waters can prove surprisingly difficult. You know the
fish are there and you can often see activity, but you cannot buy a bite. What do you
do? It's not always a case of going finer – what's the point if you're just going to lose a
good fish? Try different baits, obviously. Perhaps a cocktail, perhaps the tip of a worm.
Change your depth – come off the bottom, or even fish in mid-water. Put a couple of
handfuls of bait close in just a couple of yards or so up the bank from where you are
fishing and watch out for clouding or bubbles. Take a careful walk round the fishery
and see if there's any surface activity whatsoever. Talk to other anglers, especially
locals who know the place. Try to seek out the owner: every fishery boss wants to see
satisfied customers. Above all, don't panic – fishing is a learning experience and a
blank day can be as important as a successful one.

🌥 SEASON – open all year round.
🎣 TICKETS – these cost £3.50 and are available at the water. Contact David Bunning on
01362 820702 for further information.
➡ DIRECTIONS – from Norwich, take the B1108 to Hingham. You will soon see Cranworth
signposted on the right. Just before the village you will see a sign indicating the fishery.
🛏 ACCOMMODATION – details of accommodation can be obtained from the Norwich Tourist
Information Centre on 01603 666071.

HICKLING BROAD – NORFOLK

Every coarse fisherman had heard of the Broads, these large stillwaters dug centuries ago for supplies of peat, then filled by rain and spring water. The Broads are a shifting, fragile environment, largely because they are so close to the North Sea and subject to periodic flooding. This can lead to a boom and bust sort of situation but when the fishing is good, it can be tremendous. Perhaps the most accessible and most charming of all the Broads for the visitor is Hickling. This is a vast body of water connected with Heigham Sound – another large broad – by a deep dyke. Horsey Mere is also part of the same water complex.

Hickling is riding high at the moment, and any anglers going there can, very frequently, reap bonanza catches. There are, however, certain gold rules. For example, try to fish early and late and always make sure that you moor up – because nearly all fishing is done by boat – well away from the main cruiser channels. Ground bait thoughtfully. Fish as light as you can get away with – especially when the broad goes gin clear. Above all, manoeuvre your boat quietly and gently, and try to keep it from rocking and sending out telltale vibrations throughout the day. Use binoculars to scan the water from time to time for any signs of topping fish. This is a big water and the shoals are nomadic. If you're not catching, it could well pay to explore new areas.

I don't think we need look at any particular, special baits or methods. The bream, roach and rudd all fall to traditional baits though float fishing is probably easier than ledgering when afloat. Go for a comparatively heavy waggler that allows you to cast a good distance and still maintain control. Perch are making something of a comeback, so it pays to have a supply of lobworms with you and use one especially if you see small fish scattering before a cruising predator. There are some very, large pike and even if you are fishing for the roach and rudd, it pays to have pike gear set up with dead bait perhaps, in case there's esox activity!

The North Sea coast is close by, so the weather can be variable. North-easterly winds in the summer can bring severe chill and in the winter, watch out for northerly and easterly winds. If it's the traditional Broadland experience that you are looking for, there is no better place left to enjoy it than on the wild expanses of Hickling Broad.

SEASON – June 16th to March 14th

BOAT HIRE – Whispering Reeds Boats Ltd., Hickling, Norfolk, NR12 0YW. Phone/Fax 01692 598314.

TICKETS – these are £1 per boat and are bought from a bailiff who motors round to collect the fees. Two rods per boat are allowed.

RECORDS – there are few precise records but it is safe to assume that roach top one pound, rudd grow to two pounds and over and perch reach three pounds. Bream seem to level out around eight pounds and thirty plus pike are always on the cards. A wonderful mixed fishery. Tench can also grow large.

➡ **DIRECTIONS** – follow the Hickling Broad sign off the A149 between Potter Heigham and Stalham just to the northwest of Great Yarmouth.

🛏 **ACCOMMODATION** – Whispering Reeds offer a wide range of houseboats and cruisers. You can't beat living afloat for getting the very best out of the weather.

FRITTON LAKE – SUFFOLK

This is a beautiful and largely undiscovered water around about two and a half miles long and approaching two hundred acres in extent. It's likely Fritton was dug for its peat reserves and is, therefore, in reality a Broad rather than a lake. It averages eight to twelve feet deep – much like some of the Broads themselves – and the water too is usually well-coloured.

There are huge shoals of bream in Fritton and these are the major target for most visiting anglers. However, the roach are also widespread and run to well over the pound. There is some excellent perch fishing, a few carp and some tremendous sport is to be had with pike.

Dawn and dusk are almost certainly the best times to get down to fishing on Fritton. This is when you'll find the bream most active and really feeding hard. It pays to scan the water – preferably with binoculars – to look for any sign of rolling or priming fish. Then get to them as quickly as you can, bait up close by and wait for the fish to move over the feed. Alternatively, bait a well-known area for a day or two and then move in at first light to await your reward.

For the bream swim feeder and quiver tip is the usual approach but the roach respond well to float fished maggot or caster a couple of rod lengths out. If it's bream you're after, don't go too light because some of the fish run to a very good size indeed.

☀ **SEASON** – Fritton is now open all year with no closed season. No keep nets are allowed and no live baiting for pike.

🎣 **TICKETS** – the bailiff, Edward Knowles, can be contacted at Fritton Lake Country World, Church Lane, Fritton, Great Yarmouth NR31 9HA or phone 01493 488288. It's best to telephone beforehand to make arrangements. Tickets cost £5.20 per day for adults and £3.80 for children. You are strongly advised to book a boat for that extra mobility at £5 per day.

📖 **RECORDS** – pike are common between twenty and thirty pounds. The bream run to twelve pounds, the roach to one pound and perch of four pounds are present. Occasional carp to the mid twenties are also landed. Eel fishing is little practised but there are certainly some big specimens here.

➡ **DIRECTIONS** – Fritton is signposted off the A143 between Beccles and Great Yarmouth.

🛏 **ACCOMMODATION** – you really can't do better than stay in the holiday cottages which are available close to the lake itself. Once again, phone Mr. Knowles on 01493 488288 for details. Living on site, as it were, gives you the flexibility to really bait up for the bream shoals and make proper headway with them.

Yew Tree Lakes – Norfolk

Yew Tree rubs shoulders with some very famous waters. The two lakes here are situated in this extraordinary length of the Waveney valley between Harleston and Bungay. There's good river fishing still available if you're prepared to hunt it out but it's the pits and lakes in this area that have made angling history in the past. Waveney Valley Lakes (01986 788676) have produced big carp now for generations. The Highfield Fishery (01986 874869) holds real specimen fish. Weybread Pits have traditionally produced monsters. Homersfield Lake is another name instantly recognizable amongst specimen hunters. However, Yew Tree offers a really accessible way into this hallowed area. Many of the other waters can be difficult. I'm not saying Yew Tree doesn't offer a challenge, but it's comparatively small, feels intimate with all its features and has good fish stocks. It's a two lake complex – Yew Tree Lake is four acres and the Marsh Pool is an acre and a half. There are islands, overhanging trees and there's an undeniably fishy feel about the whole place.

I suppose what makes Yew Tree particularly exciting is the stock of catfish. Both lakes hold them, and they go to over twenty pounds. Twenty pounds might not sound a huge weight to anybody who hasn't played a catfish but, believe me, get one on the end and you'll know all about it – for the next forty minutes! There are also good carp, and both waters hold fish to around thirty pounds. Yew Tree might not quite be up to the big boys around it in terms of big fish reputation but it's getting there and it does offer a realistic chance of action.

You'll find that the catfish fight hard and doggedly. You'll need the very heaviest carp gear you've got. Remember also that they are afraid of any resistance and will drop a bait instantly if at all suspicious. They'll sometimes pick up boilies – especially fish-based ones. Try a bit of squid, a roll of anchovy or perhaps a couple of meatballs. Pepperami can work, and one of my favourites for cats is garlic sausage. Do remember that a nylon hook length isn't enough for catfish: their small rasping teeth will fray it quickly. Instead, use something abrasion-resistant such as Kryston Quick Silver.

Location is also important for catfish – even on small waters where they are plentiful. You'll often find them very close in to the bank or near to islands or lying in deeper channels. For this reason, it often pays to plumb a water before fishing, especially if you've got the time to put in a few days. Look very hard for surface activity. You'll often see the water colour as catfish begin to feed and sometimes even the tip of a tail will break surface momentarily. If you're very lucky, you will see a fish roll or even chase fry. Catfish are frequently considered nocturnal feeders but don't be put off fishing in the daytime. It's surprising how many blindingly hot afternoons will see a run develop.

One word of caution – Yew Tree is commendably harsh on litter depositors. Long-stay anglers do sometimes have something of a dubious reputation and rubbish won't be tolerated here.

☼ **SEASON** – the fishery closes between November and March.

⚔ **TICKETS** – these are £10 for four hours and can be obtained on the bank. Phone 01986 788570 for further details.

➡ **DIRECTIONS** – take the A140 from Norwich to Scole and turn onto the A143 towards Lowestoft and Bungay. At the second roundabout, turn into Wortwell Village and the lakes are well signposted on your right hand side.

⊨ **ACCOMMODATION** – the Tourist Information Centre in Lowestoft, on 01502 533600, will be able to supply details of suitable accommodation in the area.

ALTON WATER AND ARDLEIGH RESERVOIR

I'm treating these two superb waters as one entity because they are both controlled by Anglian Water and they are both prime examples of how wildlife, sailing, birdwatching and fishing can all be accommodated together in glorious surroundings. Alton is slightly to the north of Ardleigh – the first being in Suffolk and the latter in Essex – but they are very similar in feel. Both are set in green, rolling countryside and they're both approximately the same sort of size – both over a hundred acres but not so large as to intimidate an angler.

Alton was always designed as a coarse fishing water and now boasts large stocks of bream, roach, rudd and pike. It's a perfect match venue but also excellent for the visitor. The quality of fish is fantastic. The pike at Alton are getting steadily bigger: every year sees twenty pound fish as the norm and much, much bigger specimens lurk.

The same applies to Ardleigh. In fact, Ardleigh once held the British pike record with a monster of forty-four pounds. It is Ardleigh that has always attracted my own eye, possibly because it has doubled as a trout and a coarse fishery for most of its life. And we all know how pike thrive on stocked rainbows. Now, sadly, the trout fishing is being phased out, but that doesn't necessarily mean that the pike fishing will suffer as a result. The big fish still have plenty of roach and bream to sustain them. In short, I expect Ardleigh to carry on being a premier pike fishery for years to come.

But it's not just pike that make Ardleigh so special. A two pound roach is nothing in this sensational water. Bream and tench grow big, and carp are on the increase. A few years ago Ardleigh was also nationally famous for its extraordinary perch fishing and, who knows, these may well return in the same strength one day.

There's something rather liberating about fishing these waters – you know that you're in for a rewarding day. The calibre of the fish is always excellent. The birdlife is extensive. There's a feeling of openness, of freedom and you never quite know what's going to take your bait next. Believe me, the chances are there that it could be a fish to make the national headlines.

SEASON

 SEASON – Ardleigh is open all year round. At Alton, the fishing season runs from Spring Bank Holiday Saturday until 14th March the following year.

 TICKETS – for Alton ring the warden at Alton Water Treatment Works on 01473 589105. For Ardleigh, contact Barry Bartholomew, the bailiff. You can buy tickets from the fishing lodge at Ardleigh or the self-service kiosk outside the lodge. Tickets are £6 per day for an adult and £3 for juniors under sixteen years of age. Half-day tickets are also available.

 RULES – these are showcase waters where fishermen should remember to be on their best behaviour. Co-operation with sailors and birdwatchers is most important and do not fish in areas that are restricted for wildlife.

 DIRECTIONS – Alton is found just off the A137 south of Ipswich. Ardleigh is three miles outside Colchester on the A137 to Manningtree. They are so close together it is possible to take both in in a single day or certainly over a weekend.

 ACCOMMODATION – the Tourist Information Centres in Ipswich (01473 258070) and Colchester (01206 282920) can supply details of accommodation in their area.

≋ HIGHLY RECOMMENDED FISHERIES ≋

- *Decoy Lakes, Whittlesey, Cambridgeshire. Six waters here with huge heads of carp from small to around the twenty pound mark. Some roach and tench but carp are the main attraction. Tickets cost £5, contact Diane Band on 01733 202230.*
- *Middle Level Main drain, Three Holes, Upwell, Norfolk. A long straight drain controlled by King's Lynn Angling Association which holds some great pike and zander. Also good shoals of roach and bream. Good perch and also some tench. Contact Mike Grief, King's Lynn Angling Association Secretary on 01553 671545. Tickets £3.50 on the bank.*
- *Old River Nene, March, Cambridgeshire. Some great roach fishing to around about a pound with very good perch as well. Free fishing but enquire about parking and matches on 01354 658747.*
- *Gimmingham Lakes, Nr. North Walsham. Contact 01263 720432. Small lakes but very intimate with some cracking fish available – especially carp and tench.*
- *Revesby Reservoir, Lincolnshire. A thirty plus acre reservoir. Good pike, bream and tench. Plentiful small roach and perch. Red maggot and worm score well. Tickets £3 a day on the bank. At present closed season March 14th–June 16th is maintained and no fishing on Sundays. Contact 01507 568395.*

COARSE-FISHING SITES
IN THE MIDLANDS

1. Moccas Fishery
2. Docklow Pools
3. Baden Hall Fishery
4. Fisherwick Lakes
5. Packington Somers
6. Alvechurch Fisheries
7. Bishops Bowl Lakes
8. Clattercote Reservoir
9. Butlers Hill Farm
10. Blenheim Palace Lake
11. Hollowell Reservoir
12. Bluebell Fishery
13. The River Trent

'Just because I caught my record carp over on the Welsh borders and I've done a bit of pike fishing up on Loch Lomond, people tend to think of me as a great traveller, but this isn't really the case. In fact, John, I'll let you into a secret. That is, I don't really like travelling a great deal. I see this as a major bonus, living as I do in Hertfordshire. I've got all manner of waters pretty much on my doorstep and if you read my articles you'll realise that ninety-five percent of the time I'm fishing almost within casting distance of my own sitting room. I'm not saying the fishing is necessarily as good as it was when I was a lad, but there's still some really interesting sport to be found, especially if you keep your ear to the ground and you've got a network of good friends. My sneaking suspicion is that the fish themselves are probably getting bigger as the years go by. I'm not sure why this is – it could be something to do with nitrates enriching the water or perhaps increased food supplies, possibly from anglers' baits. I know you've got some great fishing close to you up in Norfolk but, I guess, on balance I'm just about as fortunate.'

LETTER FROM THE LATE RICHARD WALKER TO THE AUTHOR

Richard Walker was the greatest angler – either coarse or game – of the 20th century, and his list of big fish will probably never be equalled. There was hardly a species that he hadn't caught really breathtaking specimens of in the 1980s. And yet, Richard rarely travelled more than an hour or two from his home in Hitchin. The simple reason was, as he said, there was so much good fishing on his doorstep, so why on earth would he want to travel long distances? And he was right then, just as he would be correct now. Just think: the Ouse in Bedfordshire – home of record barbel; the Derbyshire rivers just brimming with dace; the Wye and the Severn over to the west; the reservoirs of Leicestershire; the Trent; the Meres of Shropshire; the Warwickshire Avon; the gravel pits of Oxfordshire; and, of course, the Thames.

MOCCAS FISHERY – BREDWARDINE, THE RIVER WYE

Beat six of the famous Moccas Fishery is well known among barbel anglers throughout the country. I ought to explain that the fishery is actually made up of ten beats in all, but the public are only allowed onto this one day-ticket water. Never mind – at more than a mile in extent, it offers some excellent opportunities for the specialist angler or a small club match.

The barbel are large; school fish are between six and eight pounds and there are plenty bigger than that. Above all, the fishery is widely varied, offering scope for all manner of methods. Try the deeper, slower water at the head of the beat if you want to fish static baits. From the bridge upwards, however, the quick, dancing shallows allow you to float fish or even free-line a bunch of lobs, or a dead minnow perhaps.

The pike fishing is also interesting and the chub are numerous and large. There's also the chance of a perch or two, and dace are on the comeback trail. But above all, beat six is just a beautiful place to fish, surrounded as it is by lush, rolling farmland and towering, amphitheatre-like hills.

Best times tend to be early and late (remember there is no night fishing) but barbel can be caught here throughout the day, especially if there's a bit of a tinge on the river. A careful approach makes a world of difference. Too many anglers clump to their swims, swing down heavy baskets and cast in football-size feeders. To get the best out of this water, approach with care, fish as light as you can get away with and try to do something different. That's why I mentioned worms – the natural bait approach can often work wonders here. As a final thought, don't ever fish a main line under six pounds breaking strain, as barbel fight like tigers and the winter floods bring down all manner of material to create large snags.

☀ SEASON – fishing season for barbel runs from June 16th to March 14th. Keep nets are strictly banned. Also, take great care with gates and litter here. The beat runs through pastureland and the cattle and sheep must be protected. No night fishing.

🎣 TICKETS – day tickets cost £6 and are available from Mike Taylor at the Red Lion Hotel, Bredwardine, on 01981 500303. Prior booking, though not essential, is certainly advisable, especially during busy periods.

→ DIRECTIONS – from Hereford, take the A438 Brecon road. Around ten miles from Hereford, you will see a signpost indicating Bredwardine to the left. Follow this road for a mile and a half until you reach the river bridge. The Red Lion stands another four hundred yards further on at the T-junction.

🛏 ACCOMMODATION – good accommodation can be found at the Red Lion Hotel itself – see above for details. Residents to the hotel are also allowed to fish beats one to five, an area of water excluded to day ticket purchasers. I also run barbel-fishing courses along the whole length of the Moccas Fishery. Mike Taylor will furnish dates and prices.

DOCKLOW POOLS – HEREFORDSHIRE

Docklow Pools really do represent a true labour of love: the complex is made up of an assortment of different waters, each offering a different level of challenge. Add to that some excellent accommodation and catering services on site and you really do have something a little bit special. In fact, Docklow Pools offer tremendous value for money to the holidaying angler. You've even got a well-stocked tackle shop and pub! And it's all set in beautiful countryside.

The Old Pool is ideal for children. It's attractive, safe and simply crammed with fish. Moby Dick is somewhat bigger and has a larger stamp of fish – carp, for example, go to twenty pounds plus. It's also a very appealing venue to fish, totally surrounded as it is by trees and reeds, and a place that definitely responds to the stalking, easy-does-it approach. Try fishing on the surface for the carp or close in to the margins.

⋙ STALKING FOR CARP ⋘

Most carp fishing is done in a relatively static fashion sitting behind fixed rods and baits. However, stalking can be efficient and is great fun. All you need is a rod, reel, float, hooks and bait, and off you go.

• *Always wear Polaroids – you just can't see anything without them.*

• *Only go stalking in quiet areas of the lake where you are not going to interfere with any other anglers.*

• *Look for browsing carp well away from all human activity. Remember even big fish will come into just a few inches of water. Look for them around fallen trees, weed beds and anywhere else they might feel secure.*

• *Sometimes you see the fish or its fins. At other times you'll see clouds of silt disturbed by feeding fish. Skilled stalkers can often tell the presence of carp just by the way the water stirs and rocks gently, indicating a big fish just subsurface.*

• *Stalking calls for an instant bait – try a couple of lob worms on a size 4 hook.*

• *Don't attempt to catch a carp from a swim where you know there is hardly any chance of landing it.*

• *If a fish becomes weeded, try hand lining. Point the rod straight at the problem area, hold the line tightly between the fingers and pull in a sawing motion. This will exert far more pressure than the rod can put on itself and could get the fish moving.*

• *If this does not work, let the line go slack for up to five minutes and you might find that the carp swims out of the weed or the tree root on its own accord.*

• *The best time for stalking is at dawn, when the fish are still actively roaming and feeding.*

Snake Lake is ideal for pole fishing, whereas the Figure of Eight Pool is another cracking venue for children or novices. There are also other pools at Docklow that are only open to membership tickets, and these even hold the exotic catfish. In short, membership is well worth thinking of taking out if you live locally or you think you're going to holiday in the area on a frequent basis. The countryside hereabouts is a birdwatcher's dream, the fishing is absolutely top rate and the accommodation is hard to beat.

SEASON – open all year round.

TICKETS – apply to Docklow Pools, Docklow, Nr. Leominster, Herefordshire HR6 0RU, or phone 01568 760256. Or phone the tackle shop (open in the summer) on 01568 760544. Day tickets cost £5 for adults.

DIRECTIONS – Docklow Pools is situated on the main A44 between Leominster and Bromyard. If you are travelling from Leominster, the clearly signed entrance is on the left-hand side, about four miles before reaching Bromyard.

ACCOMMODATION – there is excellent accommodation on site in either static or touring caravans, or lodges that all retain beams, sloping walls and old world charm. Alternatively, apply to the Tourist Information Centre in Leominster, on 01568 616460, for details of other accommodation in the area.

BADEN HALL FISHERY – STAFFORD

There's a really go-ahead management here at Baden Hall that has turned a promising fishery into a really exciting one. There are comprehensive club facilities and you certainly won't go short of food and drink when you're on the complex. You won't go short of fish either. Middle Pool is as nice as they come – very natural looking, and at around ten acres it holds some great fish, including double-figure bream. But there are also good carp (along with original wildies), tench to eight pounds and quality roach to over two pounds. Try maggots, worms, luncheon meat and bread. Floating bread is also a deadly method – would you believe it for the bream, I'm told! Keep nets, happily, aren't allowed on the water, so the fish are always in cracking conditions.

The Wetlands, the Match Pool and Duck Pond all provide equally satisfying fishing – each with their own particular slant and challenge. In short, there's something here for everyone. Do, however, check out the fishery rules before beginning. Keep nets, basically, are reserved for matches only, and there are restrictions on several baits. Anglers are also requested to take unhooking mats with them, especially if they are after the carp. But don't be put off. Baden really is a welcoming place and all these rules are simply designed for the good of the fish themselves, and the management should be applauded for that.

⛵ **SEASON** – open all year round from 7.00am until 9.00 in the evening and later by arrangement.

❤ **TICKETS** – contact Baden Hall Fishery, Eccleshall, Stafford ST21 6LG, or phone 01785 850313. Coarse tickets range from about £6 for adults to £3.50 for juniors.

➔ **DIRECTIONS** – from the M6, take junction 15, which is the A519, towards Eccleshall. Follow the signs to Swynnerton. Drive through Swynnerton itself, through Cold Meece and across the railway line. Go up a hill and Baden Hall is on the left, but please note that you should enter through the fishery entrance and not down the private drive.

⇥ **ACCOMMODATION** – details of accommodation available in the area can be obtained from the Tourist Information Centre in Stafford, on 01785 619619.

FISHERWICK LAKES – STAFFORDSHIRE

Fisherwick Lakes are situated in the grounds of what used to be Fisherwick Hall, though the original building has now been pulled down and all that remains is the former coach house. There are still thirty-two acres of land, in which nestle seven lakes and pools – most of them designated for coarse fishing. And there's something here for everybody. There are deep pools, shallow pools, long pools and round pools. There are pools overhung with trees and lined with thick marginal reeds. And there are the fish species – mirror carp, common carp, ghost carp, crucians, tench, bream, perch, roach, rudd, chub, golden orfe, dace and even the odd barbel – that make for a fishery where you really don't know what you're going to catch next.

At one end of the spectrum you've got waters like the Deep Hole Specimen Lake, which offers challenging fishing for carp well into the high twenties and tench to seven pounds or so in weight. Note that unhooking mats are obligatory here – excellent for the care of these very special fish. Most of the big carp are caught with mainstream methods, but there's still a real opportunity here for stalking amongst the extensive reed-beds. Also, look out for fish near the surface, especially in secluded bays.

Then you've got the Short Stream – more like a lake really, and full of fish. The water is comparatively shallow and absolutely teeming with small perch and tench, which makes it a real favourite with kids. Mind you, they could easily land a decent crucian carp, a good tench, a good mirror or even a passing chub or two.

With waters like Fisherwick it's a good idea to take your time before selecting a swim. Too many anglers are just in too great a hurry to get started, and half an hour or so spent walking the banks, looking for fish activity and deciding on a sensible approach for the day, really does pay dividends. Don't always be too keen to fish as close to your car as possible: the chances are that the more remote, peaceful areas of a fishery like this will hold the better specimens. Polaroid glasses are an excellent aid: often they'll help you actually see the fish you're hoping to catch. Also, look out for clouds of disturbed silt, twitching reeds or moving lily pads. If you are a true fishing detective, you're bound to catch more than the angler who just plonks himself down in the first available swim.

And also remember these fisheries are all about fun. You're not going to break British records and win trophies here, but fishing shouldn't be like that anyway. No, Fisherwick, and commercial fisheries like it, offer good, safe, quality fishing in very pleasant surroundings.

SEASON – open all the year round.

TICKETS – apply to Midland Game Fisheries, Fisherwick Lakes, Fisherwick Wood Lane, Whittington, Lichfield, Staffordshire WS13 8QF, or phone the Fishery Lodge on 01543 433606. The scale of charges is available from the Fishery Lodge.

DIRECTIONS – leave the A5 onto the A38 and head north towards Burton-on-Trent. Take the first turning left, signposted Lichfield Industrial Estate. At the end of the slip road, turn right. After about half a mile there is a turning on the left signposted Huddlesford. Take this and follow the lane through the countryside. Pass under the railway bridge and you will see the Plough Inn on the right hand side. Here the road splits into three. Take the middle road. After driving two miles you will come to a crossroads, and the fishery is well signposted from this point onwards.

ACCOMMODATION – the Tourist Information Centre in Lichfield, on 01543 308209, will be able to supply details of accommodation available in the area.

PACKINGTON SOMERS – WARWICKSHIRE

Over the years, Packington has built up a cracking reputation as an intimate, well-stocked and well-cared-for fishery. It offers seven pools and a three-quarter mile stretch of the River Blythe. The fishery is permanently manned, making it a haven for children – something very much in demand in this day and age. The care and control that Packington put into the fishery is immediately obvious. The banks are well tended, waters look pristine and you get the impression that the fishery is cherished. So too are the fish. Packington fish look nice, largely because keep nets are only allowed during matches and not for pleasure fishing.

There is something for everyone at Packington. The lakes make perfect match waters because they're compact and very well stocked. Some of the lakes, Molands Mere for example, are perfect for larger matches, and Molands is capable of taking well over fifty anglers with no sense of overcrowding. Then you've got Anniversaries Pool, which holds larger carp, or Willow Pool, a small, cosy water ideal for junior and disabled anglers. The water is packed with small carp, tench, roach and crucians, so a bite is by no means a rare occurrence!

Remember that when you're fishing these small waters just a few points of caution will help improve catches. Look for some feature to fish up against – islands, for example, or clumps of waterweeds. If you're fishing close in, restrict your movements and bankside vibrations. Feed carefully. And if you're fishing for smaller species such as crucians or roach, don't saturate the swim or you'll turn them off completely.

Feeding is always a problem on any water, big or small. If you're fishing for bream, you can probably get away with more ground bait than you would for roach or rudd, but always be careful not to put big balls of ground bait over a shoal's head, especially in shallow water. If in any doubt, feed less rather than more. If bites begin to tail off, this could be the sign that you've overfed the swim. Try cutting back on the feed for a quarter of an hour and then if bites don't start to materialise again start feeding once more, comparatively heavily.

SEASON – the lakes are open all year round but note that the river still has a closed season between 14th March and 16th June.

TICKETS – these are available from the Fishery Lodge, Broadwater, Maxstoke Lane, Meriden, Coventry CV7 7HR, or phone 01676 522754/523833. Summer tickets cost £5 a day and winter tickets £4 a day. There are concessions for senior citizens and juniors.

→ DIRECTIONS – Packington Somers is found south of the A45, approximately nine miles east of Birmingham and eight miles west of Coventry. Turn off the A45 at the Stonebridge island and go south on the Kenilworth Road, the A452. Turn left at the next roundabout and you will find the main entrance to the fishery, along with the Stonebridge Golf Centre, on your left.

ACCOMMODATION – the Tourist Information Centres in Birmingham (0870 599 2244) and Coventry (02476 227264) can supply details of various kinds of accommodation in the area.

ALVECHURCH FISHERIES – BIRMINGHAM

Alvechurch Fisheries, just south of Birmingham, has been a famous fishery for years and it's really on the move once more under new management. 'It is our intention and commitment to provide for anglers of all ages and ability a quality fishery and a day to remember after their visit. Our door is always open so we can listen to anglers' opinions and views , which will be taken on board. We want to provide an anglers' fishery and cannot do this without the support of the anglers themselves.' A real statement of intent from the management, and one that looks like being carried out to the benefit of local and visiting anglers alike.

The fishery is made up of four lakes and if you've got a beginner in the family you can't do better than to go to House Pool. It's relatively small and shallow but is heavily stocked with fish, as well as being truly pretty and peaceful. Small tench, rudd, roach, common and mirror carp proliferate, and the action is really hectic – great fun for all.

At the other end of the scale are Horseshoe and Arrow Pools, both holding tremendous specimens – roach to two pounds, perch to three pounds, big carp and even a few barbel, so I'm told, though I remain to be convinced. My own plea is this: if you were to latch into a barbel, please, please do not consign it to the keep net! And that goes for rivers everywhere, too.

☀ SEASON – open all year round.

🐟 TICKETS – apply to Alvechurch Fisheries, Bittell Road, Barntgreen, Birmingham B45 8LT, or phone 0121 4454274. Day tickets run from £5 for seniors to £2.50 for juniors.

➡ DIRECTIONS – from junction 2 of the M42 motorway, head towards Birmingham and Cadbury's World. At the first island, turn left towards Alvechurch. At the second island, turn right. The entrance to Alvechurch Fishery is about two hundred yards on the right.

🛏 ACCOMMODATION – the Tourist Information Centre in Birmingham, on 0870 599 2244, will be able to supply details of accommodation available in the area.

BISHOPS BOWL LAKES – WARWICKSHIRE

There's a real buzz about Bishops Bowl now it's under new management and making great strides forward again. The complex is just outside Leamington Spa, situated in a hundred acres of verdant countryside. There are five lakes, and their diversity means there's something for everyone. It's especially a great place in winter – there's a super caf and a coffee shop available that offer a great range of hot breakfasts and even bowls of chilli-con-carn for those winter afternoons when you're both freezing and famished!

Back to the fishing! Blue Pool is a flooded quarry going down to over twenty feet and holding thirty-pound-plus mirror and common carp. The depths make floater fishing a popular line of attack, but if you are fishing on the bottom, it pays to long cast against the far wall of this former quarry where the bank is inaccessible and many of the bigger fish congregate. Blue Pool has got more to offer than carp, and you'll find tench to six pounds and perch – cracking, bristling creatures – to three pounds plus.

At around three acres in size, White Bishop Lake is probably the most popular match fishery, and it holds plenty of double-figure carp, good-sized tench and quality roach. Pole fishing is a favourite method on the lake, but be careful you aren't taken by surprise by one of those good carp that wander along very frequently. Tench go well on trout pellet paste and corn. Try laying on a couple of rod lengths out and you can build up a really good day's sport.

It can pay you to look very carefully at any bubbles that break on the surface. Reading bubbles is quite an art form and will tell you the fish species that are feeding over your bait. If, for example, the bubbles are tiny and fizz on the surface, then you can be fairly sure that there are tench about. They also come up in small clusters.

If the bubbles are larger, however, and follow a mazy trail, then you've probably got a carp or two grubbing about. If you see a big cloud of silt ballooning up, and one or two very large bubbles, it could be that a group of bream have moved in. These are generalisations and there are always exceptions to the rule, but remember that pointers like this can help improve your sport.

We should mention Lodge Pool and Dinosaur Dip – two small, comparatively shallow waters situated close to the car park and ideal for disabled anglers, senior anglers and especially children. The waters are full of fish. Ideal venues for the young where you know they can fish with confidence and in safety. Children are the future of the sport and this is realised at Bishops Bowl, where they are very well looked after.

☀ SEASON – the lakes are open year round but do note that night fishing is by prior arrangement with the fishery manager on the number below.

✦ TICKETS – contact Bishops Bowl Lakes, Station Road, Bishops Itchington, Leamington Spa, Warwickshire CV33 0SR, or phone 01926 613344. Summer tickets cost £5 and winter tickets £4, with concessions for senior citizens, juniors and disabled anglers.

➡ DIRECTIONS – from junction 12 of the M40, turn right onto the B4451 to Southam. Bishops Bowl Lakes is about three miles along the road on the left. It is well signposted.

⊨ ACCOMMODATION – the Tourist Information Centre in Leamington Spa, on 01926 742762, will give advice on accommodation available in the area.

CLATTERCOTE RESERVOIR – OXFORDSHIRE

Clattercote is a feeder reservoir for the Oxford canal, with depths down to about twenty feet at the dam end and less than five feet up in the weed-strewn shallows. What makes Clattercote instantly recognizable is the wooden walkway that rings virtually the entire water, so that anglers actually sit over the water rather than on the bank. Okay, in theory this sounds artificial to the point of the ridiculous, but in practice it creates a pleasing effect and, being totally surrounded by water, you do feel that you're very much a part of the lake.

Stocking has been prolific in the reservoir. The carp go into double figures, and there are plenty of them. Tench reach about six pounds, the crucian carp are beginning to head towards two, and there is a large head of perch, roach and bream of decent sizes. In fact, this makes the ideal match water, and bags of a hundred pounds plus have so far been recorded.

Clattercote is much more than a match fisherman's water. The roach fishing goes on well throughout the winter, and in summer it's quite possible to stalk both carp and tench in the weedy shallows. The water up there is only around four or five feet deep, and you can single out individual fish if you take your time and approach carefully.

All the usual techniques work well at Clattercote, but do make sure that you don't use cereal type ground bait. Loose feeding, anyway, is all that most anglers need on the vast majority of stillwaters. Also, and I'm well behind this, keep nets are only allowed at Clattercote during matches and then two have to be provided. This is very necessary, especially if the bream are on the feed.

Clattercote is a pleasant, interesting and rapidly-improving fishery. Specimens are already appearing, and it's only going to get better, especially given the enlightened management of the place. You don't feel crowded and the walkways do give a very interesting perspective of the entire water. In short, it's a fine example of what can be done with a little imagination and a great deal of commitment.

SEASON – open all year round.

TICKETS – contact Clattercote Reservoir, Clattercote, Nr. Claydon, Banbury, Oxfordshire, or phone 01442 278717. Permits are available on the bank from the patrolling bailiff and cost £5 for an adult and £3 for senior citizens, disabled and junior anglers. Night fishing is also available, again at a cost of £5.

DIRECTIONS – leave junction 11 of the M40 motorway. Take the road for Banbury but well before the town, take the A423 signposted to Southam, which you will find on the right-hand side. About five miles down this road you will find a turning on the right signed for the Bygones Museum and Claydon. Take this, and the entrance to Clattercote is on the right about a mile down this road.

ACCOMMODATION – the closest Tourist Information Centre is in Banbury, on 01295 25999855, but the Oxford Information Centre, on 01865 726871, will also be able to give details of various kinds of accommodation available.

BUTLERS HILL FARM – OXFORDSHIRE

Situated deep down in the beautiful Cotswolds, Butlers Hill is a tremendous holiday venue for the whole family. The lovely towns nearby are excellent for shopping and browsing, whilst the pools at Butlers Hill provide entertainment for the budding angler.

Number 1 pool, once an irrigation pond for the fruit farm, holds some tremendous fish. It's only an acre but it goes down to twelve feet deep and has carp to just under thirty pounds. There are also nice surprises – grass carp, for example, and chub that go over the four-pound mark. It's a pretty lake and is well established. Fish it either on the pole or for carp with trout pellets, boilies or floaters.

Number 2 pool is shallower than number 1 but has some tremendous attractions. Roach go close to two pounds and there are also grass and ghost carp. Number 2 pool has a predominantly muddy bottom and this colours up ferociously when fish are on the feed. It's not a bad idea, therefore, to walk the circumference of the pool looking for signs before settling down to fish.

Number 3 pool is only a quarter of an acre in size and, being so intimate, is ideal for kids. It's stocked with a host of carp, roach, rudd, chub, tench and bream, and as there are very few snags, it makes for ideal fishing conditions for the inexperienced. Moreover, the pool is close to the other two, and it's shallow and secluded so children can fish on their own with a great degree of safety.

Don't expect world-shattering fishing at Butlers Hill: it's rather a gentle, interesting place to fish, full of quality specimens in lovely countryside. And you can't get much better than that, especially on a family holiday.

☀ SEASON – open all year round.

🏊 TICKETS – apply to Butlers Hill Farm, Great Roll Right, Chipping Norton, Oxfordshire OX7 5SJ, or phone 01608 684430. Day tickets are £3.50 and juniors £2.50. Night fishing is available at £5 per night but only by prior arrangement with the fishery manager. Ticket money is collected on the bank.

➡ DIRECTIONS – Butlers Hill Farm is three-quarters of the way along the A34 between Shipston on Stour and the road to Chipping Norton. Travelling south, continue through Long Compton and start up the hill as soon as you pass the village. Halfway up is a road, to the left, signed Great Roll Right. Take this and then the first left turning will have Butlers Hill Farm on the corner. Continue down the lane for two hundred yards and the entrance to the fishery car park is on the right.

🛏 ACCOMMODATION – advice on various kinds of accommodation in the area can be obtained from the Chipping Norton Tourist Information Centre on 01608 644379.

BLENHEIM PALACE LAKE – OXFORDSHIRE

Blenheim Palace Lake is stunning. It's set triumphantly in the grounds of the main house and twists and turns its way through some of the most wonderful landscaped parkland. Just to look at it, spanned by noble bridges and dotted with exquisite islands, takes the breath away. The problem with fishing Blenheim is that you can't just turn up and buy a ticket on the bank – tickets have to be booked in advance and this does need a little prior planning. But believe me, it's well worth the effort.

Fishing is by boat, and this way you can get to the most hidden little bays and mouth-watering areas. There are favourite swims, of course, but there are so many fish that it really does pay to explore and it's no real handicap being a newcomer on the water. Get there as early as you can. If you can get out before the sun is up, you will see fish on the move. The bream and tench, especially, love to give themselves away around the shallower margins. You'll spot their fins and clouds of eddying silt as they feed.

Don't get your boat too close to feeding fish or they will spook – you probably won't see them arrow off, but there will be a general decline in activity. Feed sparingly. Remember, anyway, that ground bait is banned. Simply scatter in loose feed a few yards away from the bulk of feeding fish and let them come onto it. You're always up against it if you want to ledger from a boat, although quiver-tipping is possible. Much better, and much more fitting at such a lovely water, is float fishing. Set your waggler a few inches over depth and you'll pick up both bream and tench. And who knows what else might wander along during the course of the day?

All the usual baits work very well, but try a cocktail occasionally – say sweetcorn and redworm on a size twelve, or two casters with a tiny shard of luncheon meat. Don't be afraid to experiment.

Pike fishing comes into its own from October onwards, and there really are some magnificent fish to be caught. Don't be afraid to try lures out on Blenheim, because they really do work – especially on calm, still days when you can work something close to the surface. Alternatively, try a dead bait trolled very, very slowly behind you under a float. Set the fish so it doesn't quite touch bottom and snag up all the time, and work the boat at no more than wind speed under your oars.

I fished Blenheim in July 2000 and a perfect day made me realise how privileged we anglers are to fish such a place. During the course of the day – particularly before eleven o'clock in the morning – I picked up some half a dozen tench to over five pounds and three beautiful bream. The odd roach and perch also came along. The fish fought magnificently – even the bream – and all the time there was a stunning backdrop. Blenheim is one of the places where anglers are very much on show, so do constantly be aware of that. Remember that loud voices and bad language travel particularly well across the water.

☀ **SEASON –** Blenheim is closed from March 14th to June 16th.

🐟 **TICKETS –** these must be booked in advance from the Blenheim Estate Office. Phone 01993 811432. You will be sent a provisional booking letter and form. You will need to fill this in, make out your cheque, and return it. Your permits and instructions will be sent on to you. One angler and boat costs £25 for the day and two anglers and a boat cost £30 for the day. You can book three anglers into a boat but this does tend to get uncomfortable.

➡ **DIRECTIONS –** take the A44 north out of Oxford. This passes through the village of Woodstock, and Blenheim Palace is impossible to ignore on your left hand side. The actual instructions to the anglers car park will be given on your permit.

🛏 **ACCOMMODATION –** there is a great deal of hotel, guesthouse, and bed and breakfast accommodation in the area, including Woodstock itself. Contact the Tourist Information Centres in Woodstock on 01993 813276 or Oxford on 01865 726871 for details.

HOLLOWELL RESERVOIR – NORTHAMPTONSHIRE

Hollowell is one of those rare finds – a really prolific reservoir fishery where big fish can be taken in enough numbers to make it not too much of a specialist game. Hollowell is attractive too. Set in rolling countryside, it's a good-sized water at a hundred and forty acres, rarely gets crowded and always offers a feeling of peace and space.

Hollowell has been making the news for many years now, ever since its extraordinary roach-rudd hybrids appeared. These fabulous creations, often weighing over three pounds in weight, look sensational and fight like fiends. But that's not all

Hollowell has to offer. There are tench up to eight pounds, and huge shoals of bream between five and twelve pounds in weight. The carp also do well. The record common is a monster of nearly thirty-five pounds and the mirrors go well over twenty. Feeder fishing with maggot, caster, corn and boilies is the traditional way of fishing at Hollowell but it is possible to float fish, especially where there is deeper water close in.

Part of the reason for these stunning big fish weights is the fact that Hollowell is a very fertile environment. The silty bed of the water is heavily colonised with bloodworm, shrimp, beetle and corixa, and so the natural larder is a full one. Considering this fertility, it is not surprising that weed growth can be heavy, and it sometimes pays to fish early or late in the year, especially if you're using swim feeder tactics at long range.

It wouldn't be fair to leave Hollowell without a mention of the pike fishing. The pike are prolific, feasting on a diet of smaller fish. They are also large, and twenty-five-pound-plus specimens are caught frequently. The fishing really takes off in the late autumn when the weed growth dies back to allow you to drift float a dead bait away from the bank and explore distant features. Always remember when dead baiting, though, to take a pair of binoculars with you so that you can see a take very early on. Strike at once, or you risk deep hooking when the range is eighty yards or more.

SEASON – the fishery opens on 1st April and closes on 28th February. Note that night fishing is not available on a day ticket but is restricted to season permit holders.

TICKETS – for all bookings and advise on ticket prices, contact the Fishery Warden on 01604 781350, or c/o Pitsford Water, Holcot NN6 9SJ.

DIRECTIONS – Hollowell Reservoir is on Guilsborough Road, Hollowell, Northants. Hollowell itself is easy to find. It is seven miles north of Northampton, just off the A5199 and A14 motorway link.

ACCOMMODATION – the Tourist Information Centre in Northampton, on 01604 622677, will be able to supply details of suitable accommodation in the area.

BLUEBELL FISHERY – NORTHAMPTONSHIRE

Bluebell Fishery is nationally famous for its Kingfisher Lake, which has produced a whole array of very serious carp, including fish of over forty pounds. There are also very big catfish, huge grass carp, and bream and tench both well into double figures. Bluebell Lake, supposedly easier than Kingfisher, is also a prime big-fish venue that also holds big mirrors and large bream, along with tench, golden orfe to four pounds, and perch and crucian carp, both of which top three pounds, as well. With roach to two pounds plus and eels to seven and a half pounds, you can see that this is a very serious fishery indeed. There's also Wood Pool, which is a more run-of-the-mill match water. There are also a couple of miles of the River Nene, a stretch that can produce carp to thirty pounds, big bream and very good chub, along with tench, perch and roach. So, as you can see, there's something for everyone at Bluebell. And I haven't even mentioned the pike! Sand Marten and Swan Lakes hold specimens to over thirty pounds, and are regular venues for Pike Anglers' Club events.

Of course, waters as successful as this do not yield up their prizes easily, and it pays to take time out to plan a successful approach. Don't rush to the first available swims. Think carefully about bait, rig and loose feed. Go the boily route by all means, but don't neglect float fishing in the margins or floater fishing in calm bays. Kingfisher Lake is very weedy in the summer and so you have to take this into account. It's no good casting a heavy lead into thick weed, because your bait will simply be hidden. Look for those areas where weed is at its thinnest, perhaps on the top of bars for example, where water fowl can keep patches clear. Or fish with suspended baits – pop-up boilies or maggots glued to a cork ball. Don't neglect natural baits: worms, especially lobs and brandlings, work very well at the complex for all species of fish. It's sad that lobworms have disappeared from the carp angler's list of bait these days, because for many years they were hugely successful and would be again, given a decent run. Take note of the wind – if at all possible, fish with it in your face. Don't neglect the margins – the fish here are great patrollers and are looking for food close in. In short, fish with as open a mind as possible and don't be afraid to experiment if you want to get the very best out of this fascinating complex of waters.

SEASON – open all year round, twenty-four hours a day.

TICKETS – apply to Bluebell Fishery, Tansor, Nr. Oundle, Northamptonshire PE8 5HN, or phone 01832 226042. There is a whole scale of charges depending on the water in question and whether night fishing is included. Prices start at about £15 for an all-night ticket and go down to less than £3 for a river half-day ticket.

DIRECTIONS – on the main A14 take the A45/A605 junction at Thrapston. Follow the A605 north towards Titchmarsh, Oundle and Peterborough. Continue along this road for several miles until you pass a turning to Oundle on the left. A little further on, again on the left, is a turning for Tansor. Drive through the village and, as you leave it and head into the countryside, the white railings marking the entrance to Bluebell Lakes can be seen on the left. The drive to the fishery is a mile through the fields.

ACCOMMODATION – the Tourist Information Centres in Oundle, on 0870 1515500, and Peterborough, on 01733 452336, will be able to supply details of various kinds of accommodation in the area. Caravans and tents are catered for on the fishery site.

THE RIVER TRENT – MIDLANDS

The Trent is the largest river system in England, rising in Staffordshire, crossing the country west to east, and emptying into the Humber. Years ago, fishing in the Trent was severely hit by pollution, but it recovered and, during the 1970s and 1980s, hit unprecedented successes. At the start of the 21st century, fishing

has become difficult and some doubts have been voiced as to whether the fish are simply hard to catch or are no longer there.

However, the Trent remains a cracking river and it's simply the case that certain matches are fished in the wrong conditions at the wrong time of the day and therefore the wrong impression has been given. In fact, there are huge barbel and chub still to be caught throughout the Trent. Double-figure barbel are not unknown, and chub to well over six pounds exist.

It's probably true to say that there are two main attacks on the Trent. Firstly, you can use a stick float close in with single or double caster or bronze maggot on light tackle. Don't be afraid to change baits when bites begin to slow down. Bread, a redworm, the tip of a lobworm or even stewed wheat can work well. They can easily produce an unexpected large barbel as well. You're more likely, however, to catch roach and the smaller chub and bream for most of the day. Nonetheless, if you've built up some feed, expect the barbel and bigger chub to move in as the light fails.

It's fair to say that most big fish still come to quiver-tip and feeder techniques. For big fish, don't be afraid to experiment. Spice up your feed – the commercially bought ground baits all work well, but try introducing chopped worms, crushed trout pellets, crushed hemp, minced meat or pulped meatballs. In winter especially, when there's a tinge to the river, a good smell is vital.

Similarly, experiment with your hook baits. Double lobworm, a huge knob of cheese paste, two or even three meat balls on a hook length, a strip of bacon, half a sprat – anything that makes a big barbel or chub sit up and take notice. Of course, most fish will continue to come on triple bronze maggot, perhaps, on a size fourteen hook, but that doesn't mean to say that you can't play different options.

Think about your tackle, too. A swim feeder, either open or block-end, is the most common form of attack, but there are times when a straight lead will be an advantage. Fish do wise up to the feeder, and a lead can help allay suspicions. Also, if you're going for a big, bold bait, you don't need quite as much loose feed around.

Think carefully about where you're going to fish the feeder. Sometimes the deeps of mid river are where you'll want to fish, but there are other occasions when trees on the far banks, for example, should hold your attention. Remember that if you're fishing at range, a flat lead is going to hold bottom much better than anything else.

Think hard about the conditions. In summer, if the water is clear, there's not a great deal of point fishing during the heat of the day. Try and get out very early, around dawn, and stay till breakfast time. Alternatively, arrive at teatime and fish till the last knockings.

The same applies in winter if water conditions are clear, but if they're murky and there's a good flood on, fish can be caught throughout the day. It's probably better to arrive about noon when the water temperature is at its highest and then have a concentrated attack for the last four or five hours or so. That way you don't get too cold and your concentration doesn't disappear.

There are times in the winter when you just have to be out on the river. If there's been a period of warm, damp weather with air temperatures consistently between eight and eleven degrees it's criminal not to be on the riverbank. You'll find that all fish species fish well during this period and you can even pick up a bonus big barbel or two. A winter carp is also very much on the cards.

☀ SEASON – open June 16th to March 14th.

✚ TICKETS – there is a huge amount of access open to the visiting angler along the Trent. In fact, the vast majority of this huge river is available on day ticket and a good amount of this is simply payable on the banks. Expect to pay between £3 and £5 for a cracking day's sport. Robert Hardy, on 01636 525265, is a good contact. Robert controls a great stretch of the Trent at East Stoke in Nottinghamshire, not far from Newark. The Nottingham and District Federation of Angling Societies also controls huge amounts of river. Write to W. Belshaw, 17 Spring Green, Clifton Estate, Nottingham. Also contact the Nottingham Anglers' Association via I. Foulds, 95 Ilkeston Road, Nottingham. Scunthorpe and District Angling Club, on 01652 655849, also controls good water in the tidal stretches. Newark is also a great centre. Contact the Newark and District Piscatorial Federation on 01636 702962. The Worksop and District Anglers' Association, on 01909 485176, also has good water in the area. The Nottingham Piscatorial Society has good water around Rolleston in Nottinghamshire. Contact them on 01623 759589. In Nottingham itself there is good mixed fishing, and several miles of the river is free within the city. The Midland Angling Society, on 0115 9634487, has good water at Thrumpton. In Staffordshire, contact the Stone and District Angling Society on 01785 819035. In Stoke, the Stoke City and District Angling Association, on 01782 267081, has a whole list of fishing in the area.

🛏 ACCOMMODATION – the Tourist Information Centres in Stafford, on 01785 619619, Nottingham, on 0115 9155330, and Lincoln, on 01522 579056, can all supply details of suitable accommodation in your chosen area.

❧ HIGHLY RECOMMENDED FISHERIES ❧

- *Himley Park, Dudley, West Midlands. Good tench, excellent crucians, carp and, notably, grass carp. A really great setting. Tickets £4 on the bank. Phone 01902 324093.*
- *Larford Lake, Stourport, Worcestershire. Nearly thirty acres. Big bream, roach and tench. Good perch fishing with crucians and some good carp. Also included is two miles of the River Severn with barbel, chub, dace and roach. Day tickets cost £5. Contact Arthur Field on 0374 703067.*

- *Chasewater, Brownhills, Staffordshire. This is set in Chasewater Country Park, a very pleasant setting. It is a large water with great roach fishing and some very good perch. Also some good pike. Tickets at £2.20 are available on the bank. Contact the Ranger on 01543 542302.*
- *The River Avon, The Lido, Stratford, Warwickshire. A good stretch of the Avon just outside Stratford offering excellent chub, plentiful roach and dace. There are also some decent bream and a few barbel. A good winter fishery after heavy rain. Waggler, stick float and swim feeder all work well. Day tickets £1.80 on the bank. Contact Dave Jones' Angling Centre, Stratford, on 01789 293950, for bait and up to the minute advice on conditions.*
- *The Erewash Canal, Dockholme, Nottinghamshire. A really steady venue with plenty of fish including chub to around three pounds, roach, skimmers, perch and some big carp. Try caster and worms for the larger fish, with meat for the carp. A good winter fishery but fishes well all year. Tickets cost £2. Contact Eric Aynsworth of Long Eaton Federation on 01159 256270 for further details.*
- *Earlswood Lakes, Earlswood, Warwickshire. This is worth mentioning as it is just south of Birmingham and the complex offers some great fishing. Plenty of fish and some really good specimens. Good pike, for example, to around the twenty-pound mark. Note there is no live baiting. Also famous for eels. Tickets cost £5. Contact John Howse on 01217 834233.*
- *Hooly Farm Fishery, Ashby Magna, Leicestershire. Three characterful lakes here. Tremendous match waters with plenty of fish for everybody. Also included are some splendid exotics such as golden tench. Tickets cost £4. Phone 01455 202391 for further details.*
- *Rolf's Lake, Holton, Oxfordshire. A really attractive, matured venue. Carp, tench, bream, roach, big chub and occasional golden orfe. Note that fishing is only available by prior arrangement. Contact Rolf Wobbeking on 0802 708937.*
- *Rudyard Lake, Staffordshire. A lovely lake – I caught my first bream here. Very good pike fishing, plenty of roach and bream, and reputedly some very big perch. Phone 01538 306 280.*
- *Milestone Fisheries, Gloucestershire. A big pike water – live baits available on site. A small coarse lake with big bream and very decent carp. Phone 01285 713908 for further details.*
- *Chad Lakes, Bleddington, Gloucestershire. This is an excellent commercial fishery opened back in the mid 1990s, holding good carp, tench, bream and roach. All usual methods and baits – try floating baits for carp in the summer. Bream, apparently, to seven pounds and roach to over a pound and a half. Close to Stow on the Wold – an excellent shopping centre. Tickets available on the bank, or contact Dave Wren on 01451 831470. No keep nets.*

COARSE-FISHING SITES
IN WALES

1. Anglesey Lakes
2. The River Dee
3. Llangollen Canal
4. The River Teme
5. The River Irfon
6. The River Wye
7. Llangorse Lake
8. Pembrokeshire Fishing
9. Half Round Pond
10. Darren Lake

I just love being down here in Wales even though I was lucky enough to live for many years right by the Avon. Even that doesn't compare with the fishing I've got hereabouts. Of course, the Wye is special, you know that, but there are all manner of little places tucked here and there around this fabulous country. And what countryside it is. It never ceases to amaze me just how secretive some of the valleys are. And you never quite know what's going to happen. For example, this morning I woke up and there was snow on the ground. I walked outside and found that the Wye was still running low and clear. Or at least I think it was. Believe it or not, it was frozen for at least seven-eighths of the way across. Needless to say there wasn't much to be caught, although I did pick up a few grayling. Wales is a wild, wonderful place. If you can't live here, then at least try it for a holiday.

BOB JAMES, AUTHOR, TV STAR AND BEDROCK OF THE ACA, ON THE PHONE TO THE AUTHOR

I lost my own heart to Wales many years ago when my fishing club up in Lancashire used to make its annual journeys to the River Dee. I'd never fished a river that was so clear and so quick-flowing. And, until those days on the Dee, I'd never come across dace. What beautiful, silver, dart-like fish they are.

Other favourite fish here? The grayling are crackers and again tend to be overlooked. Most of the game fishermen spend their life after trout, salmon or, especially, sea trout. The coarse fishers tend to concentrate on carp, pike, tench and barbel. That leaves grayling in a vacuum, ignored by both camps. What a mistake!

There's also brilliant chub fishing, often in rivers that have hardly ever been fished. This is marvellous, creepy-crawly sort of stuff that takes you back to the days of childhood. Yes, Wales is very much a land for the explorer: you'll find secretive pools and small streams if you look hard enough. Okay, some are private but with a bit of investigation and politeness you never know what doors might open to you.

ANGLESEY LAKES

Anglesey is one of the country's major tourist attractions, but those holiday-makers flooding along the A5 needn't only think about buckets and spades! There is now some very appealing coarse fishing available on Anglesey. It's not on the grand scale, and don't expect to see yourself featuring on the front page of the angling press. That's not what Anglesey is about. Rather it offers some very appealing small stillwaters, generally set in super locations. And, most importantly, there's frequently a great deal for the family to do in the area. Anglesey has plenty of hotels, bed and breakfast, and guest houses. For general information about accommodation on the island, contact the Tourist Information Centre in Holyhead on 01407 762622.

CWM RESERVOIR

This is a two-acre reservoir only a short way outside the town of Holyhead. It's picturesque and is close the South Stack landmark – well worth visiting in its own right. Stocks are dense: you can hope to catch carp, rudd, bream, perch, roach and tench. Individual sizes aren't great but you can expect bites throughout the day, which makes it a great water for the family. Please not that, in common with most of the waters on Anglesey, barbless hooks are obligatory, and don't use a keep net unless you are fishing in a match. The glorious Anglesey rudd is particularly susceptible to the chafing of net mesh.

⛱ SEASON – the lake is open all the year round, dawn till dusk.
🎟 TICKETS – these cost £3 per day and are available from the Tackle Bar Shop, William Street, Holyhead. Further information can be obtained on 01407 765479 or 01407 860239.
➜ DIRECTIONS – in Holyhead, take the minor road west toward South Stack Cliffs. You need the signposts for Llaingoch and South Stack opposite the Cambria pub. After a quarter of a mile or so, you will see the turning to the reservoir on the right.

LLYN BRYNTIRION

Bryntirion is a working farm situated down in southwest Anglesey, so it's perfect for the whole family. There is always something going on and always animals to feed. The fishing isn't bad, either! There are three ponds offering prolific carp fishing and some splendid perch. The carp don't grow large but their numbers make it ideal for a family outing. Perch, though, are reputed to be serious. There are certainly two-pounders and the place calls for a bit of investigation. Fish a lobworm on a size four hook, and you stand a good chance of picking up either a good carp or a cracking stripy! A really good venue for all the family.

⛱ SEASON – the lake is open from March through to October. Note that fishing times run from 8.00am until dusk.

TICKETS – these cost £3 a day and are available from Mr Naylor, Bryntirion Working Farm, Dwyran, Anglesey LL61 6BQ, or phone 01248 430232.

DIRECTIONS – from Bangor, take the A5 across the Britannia Bridge and turn off on the A4080, following the signs to Brynsiencyn. In the village, follow the road to the right and the brown signs to the Working Farm.

LLYN DEWI

This is another small but very attractive water, absolutely packed with fish. You'll find carp into double figures and some superb rudd fishing. The rudd is, as it were, the national fish of Anglesey and you won't really find better specimens anywhere else in the country. It doesn't matter how big a rudd is – it's a beautiful fish! Try for them on the surface with tiny bits of floating bread. Or catapult maggots out letting them sink slowly and then fish a shotless float rig in the area. You'll find that rudd love to come up off the bottom to intercept baits in mid water and above.

SEASON – open all year round.

TICKETS – these cost £4 and are available from Mr Hughes, Fferam Uchaf, Llanddeusant, Anglesey, or phone 01407 730425.

DIRECTIONS – From the A5, turn right, signposted Bodedern. Go through the village and take the signs for Valley. After the 30mph-limit sign, take the first turning right and follow the road down to Llanddeusant. Follow the Llanbabo road and Llyn Dewi is between one and two miles along the road. It is signposted.

LLYN Y GORS

This really is one of the star lakes of Anglesey, situated just outside Beaumaris. There is some wonderful water here with excellent fish stocks – carp, catfish, rudd, tench, roach, perch, golden orfe and bream – and that's not mentioning the tremendous stock of ghost carp, another favourite on Anglesey. The carp certainly exceed twenty pounds and the catfish are rumoured to be doing well. But it's a big bag venue in essence. There's a match lake, recently opened, and stocked to the hilt. This is definitely a place for the holidaying angler, probably with a couple of mad-keen youngsters at his or her side. Action is guaranteed.

SEASON – the fishery is open all year round, 7.30am to dusk. There is a shop on site.

TICKETS – these cost £8 a day and are available from Roger Thompson, Llyn Y Gors, Llandegfan, Menai Bridge, Anglesey LL59 5PN, or phone 01248 713410.

DIRECTIONS – take the A5 over the Britannia Bridge and follow the flyover towards Benllech. Go straight ahead at the Four Crosses public house roundabout and follow the road towards Beaumaris. Turn right before Pentraeth garage. Keep left towards Beaumaris through Hen Llandegfan. You will see the sign to the fishery on the right after the village.

ACCOMMODATION – contact the Tourist Information Centre in Holyhead on 01407 762622.

Ty Hen

This is a brilliant water – quite small at one and a half acres, but fed with natural spring water, which gives the place its own life and lustre. The place is very well stocked with common, mirror and ghost carp. Twenty-pounders have reputedly been caught. There are also some cracking tench going well above six pounds. It's a comparatively new lake – about twenty years or so – but is well matured. There's an island that attracts many of the carp, especially during hot, still, summer days. Please note that barbless hooks are the rule here and no keep nets are allowed.

☀ Season – fishing begins on 21st March and runs through to the 30th October. Dawn till dusk.
⚓ Tickets – these costs £5 a day with an evening ticket of £3. Apply to B. J. Summerfield, Ty Hen, Rhosneigr, Anglesey LL64 5QZ, or phone 01407 810331.
➡ Directions – driving along the A5, turn left after Gwalchmai onto the A4080 to Rhosneigr. Turn sharp right before Llanfaelog Post Office. Drive a mile along this road and you will find the entrance to the fishery a hundred yards on the left after the railway station.
🛏 Accommodation – there is accommodation on site.

Tyddyn Sargent

This is only a one-and-a-half-acre lake but it's attractive and well stocked. There's a good head of carp, generally quite small but easy to catch, along with roach, rudd, tench and bream. There are crucian carp and some very attractive ghost carp that give the fishery a real feeling of the exotic.

☀ Season – all the year round. Note barbless hooks only. No keep nets.
⚓ Tickets – these cost £5 a day. Contact K. Twist, Tyddyn Sargent, Tynygongl, Nr. Benllech, Anglesey, or phone 01248 853024.
➡ Directions – from Bangor, take the A5 express way into Anglesey. Turn up the slip road signposted Benllech and turn right at the roundabout. Go straight ahead to the village, where you will come to a crossroads. Turn left, signposted Llangefni. Continue for a mile and then turn right, signposted Llanfair ME. Turn right after the telephone box and Tyddyn Sargent is the second house on the left. Drive through the gates to the parking area.

Grayling Fishing in Wales

If you want to sample some real wild Welsh fishing, how about pursuing grayling, especially in the autumn when the brown trout fishing has finished? Some of my best days have been spent searching for these delightful fish on both fly and bait. Welsh grayling really are the world's best-kept secret: there are big grayling available in Wales, at least as large as those from the Wessex chalk streams. The only reason that the angling fraternity doesn't really know about these fish is that they haven't been extensively investigated.

Whether you're fishing for the grayling with fly or bait, my advice is to be mobile. Okay, you'll sometimes settle on a deep pool that proves to be full of fish, and you'll catch one after another, all day long. But this is rare. Mostly, you'll find grayling scattered along a length of river in small groups of perhaps ten or fifteen fish. Catch a couple and you'll scare the rest – you've just got to move on.

Long-trotting techniques are as good as any when it comes to locating fish on stretches of river that you're not sure about. Perhaps a couple of brandlings on a size fourteen under a buoyant, highly visible float add up to the best approach. A twelve- or thirteen-foot rod, three-pound line straight through to the hook, and you're in business. Simply long-trot every glide you come across and look for that float shooting away. If you do hook a fish, keep your rod low to avoid the grayling splashing, and try to hustle it out of the area before it disturbs its shoal members. You'll find that a one-and-a-half-pound grayling puts up a real struggle in a quick river – in fact you could well think you've got a four-pound chub on the end, which isn't an impossibility!

If you're fishing worm, you probably won't be able to get away with a barbless hook, but just dampen the barb down a little bit and try to unhook all grayling in the water. If you think grayling fight hard in the water, wait till you try and touch them! They squirm like an eel and do themselves no good at all.

The only time you're likely to come across real concentrations of grayling is towards the end of their season in March, when they are grouping ready for spawning. If you do hit into these huge shoals, take a few fish and then move on. It's not fair to hammer fish near their spawning beds.

Bait fishing for grayling is not universally allowed, so do check very carefully when you buy your permit. Ensure also what bait restrictions are in place. For example, the most commonly-banned bait is the maggot. This isn't an attempt to be difficult – it's simply trying to protect the stocks of salmon parr in any water. If there is a problem, don't neglect a piece of sweetcorn. Grayling love the yellow grains and they are pretty well parr-proof. Also, make sure that you are fishing within the prescribed limits. On some of the wilder rivers, it's all too easy to wander into a restricted beat. This is some of the most glorious fishing that Wales has to offer, but remember that you can get coarse fishermen a bad name unless you stick to the rules.

Before moving on to the logistics, let me just put in a little plea here for fly fishing. It could well be that you've been a bait fisherman all your life and have disregarded fly fishing altogether. I honestly believe that you are making a mistake here. Fly fishing is not difficult – fly casting can certainly be learnt in half a day – nor does it need to be expensive. You can kit yourself out for well under a hundred pounds, and day tickets for autumn and winter grayling in Wales, as in many parts of the country, are very cheap indeed. So, if you are a keen freshwater fisherman, do think about taking up the fly rod. It will give you immense pleasure and open all manner of doors. Remember, too, that all sorts of coarse fish can be taken on the fly – perch especially are suckers for a big, flashy lure. Fly fishing for pike is becoming more and more popular and I personally am beginning to master the techniques of catching barbel on a nymph. Believe me, there's no more exciting way of catching these sporting fish.

⛅ **SEASON** – note that the grayling is out of season between March 14th and June 16th. It is often difficult to secure grayling tickets, however, before the end of the trout season in October. Fortunately the grayling bites well in the coldest of weather.

🐟 **TICKETS** – many of the best grayling stretches are on protected waters, but day ticket possibilities do exist. One of the most exciting is in Llangollen, where the Llangollen Angling Association has fourteen miles of water, much of which can be bait fished. Tickets are available from S. Hughes, Newsagents, 12 Chapel Street, Llangollen, or phone 01978 860155. Also on the Dee, contact Derek Cycles on 01978 821841. You could also try the Tytandderwen Farm stretch near Bala – contact Mr Davis on 01678 520273.

For the River Wye, contact Mike Morgan of the Groe Park and Irfon Angling Club in Builth Wells, on 01982 552759. The club offers water upstream of the bridge in the town. There is some good grayling fishing along several hundred yards of streamy water. Some of the fish can grow big.

You could also contact Peter Smith at the Caer Beris Manor Hotel on 01982 552601. There is a mile or more of private water, the River Irfon, running through the grounds of the hotel, and there is some excellent grayling fishing in the pools. Fishing is primarily for hotel guests, and the accommodation is superb.

Just outside Wales, at Ludlow, flows the River Teme with some good grayling trotting water. Phone Ludlow Tackle on 01584 875886. There is also free fishing on the town water in Ludlow downstream of Dinham Bridge. This beat extends for approximately one and a half miles, and is good trotting water.

LLANGOLLEN CANAL

This canal is an absolute delight, almost unique in my experience. Your access is likely to be in the busy town of Llangollen itself, which is all of a bustle from spring through to autumn, but once you've walked away out into the countryside, the whole scene changes dramatically. In fact, this can be like coarse fishing on a southern chalk stream, so clear runs the water. Yes, runs. Through the canal there's a constant flow of water seeping in from the Dee itself, the river that marks the beginning of the canal.

Roach and bream are the prime targets, and what fish they are – especially the roach. Groups of fish of way over a pound and nudging the two-pound mark are quite visible to the angler who stalks them carefully in good light conditions with Polaroid glasses. The bream, too, respond to this approach, and you'll often see patches of water muddied by their feeding.

But how to approach these really super canal species? My advice is to fish as light as possible with tiny baits and just a scattering of loose feed. I remember one morning around about a mile from the town where I took four bream to five pounds on just a tiny pinch of breadflake with an anchoring SSG shot eight or nine inches up the line. Bites were infinitesimal. The line would simply tighten minutely or shake as though a breeze had caught it. Each time I struck, a big bream was wallowing in water just a couple of feet deep.

The same sort of technique works for roach – a caster or a couple of maggots, on a size eighteen perhaps, flicked under a far bank bush or into the deeper water where the canal occasionally narrows.

The angler who stays put isn't likely to catch a great deal, because the shoals of fish can be very nomadic, especially during the day when the passenger barges are being pulled up and down the canal with sickening (for the angler) regularity. Fish aren't stupid, though, and they soon get used to the disturbance. In short, I find there is something totally magical about this canal and, with its challenging fishing and superb roach and bream, it's a treasure of a venue.

SEASON – this is now a year-round fishery.
TICKETS – the Northwest Region of British Waterways has introduced the Waterway Wanderers Permit to cover most of the canals in their region. Tickets are obtainable at £10 a season or £1.50 a day. Contact Northwest Region, Navigation Road, Northwich, Cheshire CW8 1BH or phone 01606 723800.
DIRECTIONS – you'll find the canal in the centre of Llangollen, close to the station. It then winds its way through the town into the countryside towards the Dee itself. You can't miss it.
ACCOMMODATION – Llangollen is very much a holiday town with, many bed and breakfasts, guesthouses and hotels. The Royal Hotel, on 01978 860202, by the river bridge is personally recommended. Alternatively, contact the Tourist Information Centre in Llangollen on 01978 860828.

THE RIVER WYE

Now I know that the River Wye is traditionally regarded as an English river, but in my heart I feel it's Welsh, and in the general layout of this book I feel it is perfectly logical to include it here in the Welsh section as well as in the Midlands section (see page 66).

A little history might not go amiss here. For most of the 20th century, the Wye was one of the country's leading salmon rivers. If we look back to the 1920s, catches were legendary. Salmon were not only prolific – they were huge. Thirty-pounders were commonplace, and forties were caught each and every year. This meant that for whole decades, coarse fishing on the Wye was rendered next to impossible as nearly all the beats were private and fished for salmon. Okay, here and there, in the town centres especially, coarse fishermen could be accommodated and there have always been big catches of chub, perch and pike with roach further down river.

However, it was only from the 1990s and with the tragic decline of the salmon stocks that a little water began to trickle onto the coarse market. It would still be a mistake to think that there is a lot of coarse fishing available on the Wye but the amount is increasing annually. And what fishing it is.

We are primarily talking about chub fishing, which can be splendid. All the usual methods work and you will find huge numbers of fish between three and five pounds in weight. I've often been sceptical about the legendary monsters of the Wye, but in recent years there have been more fish of six pounds turning up, with at least one genuine seven-pounder recorded. Why not try floating crust in the summer? Throw twenty or thirty pieces in and simply follow them downriver until they're attacked. You can be quite sure they will be attacked before long!

Pike fishing is also excellent in the Wye and is frequently ignored. Of course, one of the great benefits of the Wye is that there are so many sanctuary areas for the fish. If the pike feel pressurised in one area, they can simply move up- or downriver until they slip away into the unknown – very easy, as so much of the Wye bankside is heavily wooded and impenetrable.

❧ Barbel On A Float ❧

Most barbel are caught on swim feeders or leads, but float fishing can be great fun. Choose a meaty rod, a minimum of 12 feet in length.

- *Centre pins are ideal for the job.*
- *Main line ought to be around about 6 pounds breaking strain.*
- *Choose a float that is well up to job. There is no point in going too light or you will struggle with control.*
- *An Avon-type float is ideal for streamy water. A big stick float will suffice if the flow is more placid.*
- *It generally pays to fish quite a way over depth so that the bait is dragging bottom – exactly how the barbel expect to find it.*
- *If you are fishing over depth, then a long trot is not possible. Instead, try to work up the five or so yards of water in front of you. Fish this neatly, tightly and the barbel should come.*
- *Don't worry too much about differentiating between a bite and the shot catching on the bottom – a bite will generally pull the rod out of your hands! At the least, you will certainly know about it.*
- *Loose feed tightly and consistently – for example, ten or so grains of sweetcorn each cast, or a small handful of maggots. Make sure that the bait is getting down to the riverbed in the right place. It is no good baiting the next swim downriver.*

Lure fishing works very well when the water is clear, and in flood time, search out the bays with dead bait. Don't expect twenty-pounders each and every visit, but they're there in good numbers and a thirty-pounder is always on the cards, especially at the back end. As ever, treat your pike with the greatest respect and care, and don't let a big fish flop around on a hard bank and injure itself. Flatten down the barbs on those lure trebles. If you're dead baiting, strike quickly once a bite develops. Don't delay the strike: if you miss a take, then in all probability it's a jack pike and of no interest. A big fish will almost certainly be hooked.

There are other treats, too. Perch seem to be coming back – at least in the middle Wye, which I personally know best. Dace stocks are also recovering, and trotting with maggot can give you a tremendous autumn day's sport – in the summer the minnows probably tend to be too prolific to even think of using maggot as bait! You'll find bream here and there, and even the odd wandering carp. But, above all, the Wye is now gaining a huge reputation for its barbel stocks.

Barbel haven't been in the river very long – perhaps twenty years or so – and they're not well established throughout the river but are still found in pockets. Mind you, those pockets are now extending rapidly, and much of the middle Wye is now a barbel fisher's paradise – providing, of course, that access can be gained.

The Wye is generally low and clear in the summer and this allows for stalking techniques. Walk your stretch of river very carefully with Polaroids, looking for any of the giveaway signs. Flashing fish, rolling fish and even jumping fish are quite common. Try and get out at dawn and perhaps you will see barbel working on the shallows. Don't rush this side of the business: barbel aren't spread randomly like currants through a cake on the river Wye and you need to locate their swims.

Once located, the barbel tend to be somewhat less pressured than on many typical English rivers. This means that you can often get away with more clumsy tactics than you would want to employ on, say, the River Kennett. This does not mean they are stupid and that they don't learn quickly, because they do. Still, the fact remains that in many areas you can still catch barbel on sweetcorn and feeders. And let me make a plea here. The barbel of the Wye, in places, are naive and can be caught comparatively easily. If you do happen on a near-virgin shoal of barbel, please don't hammer them. Take two or three fish and then leave them alone. That way you can come back to them over and over again over many seasons without disturbing them too greatly and pushing them up the ladder of knowledge.

If you've been used to the river in low summer conditions, don't be too frightened when autumn comes and the river rises dramatically. It might look very scary, but you can still catch barbel. They do tend to push out of the main flows to some degree, but don't just look for slack water. The barbel is shaped to hug bottom in pretty quick currents, and if you can hang a bait out a few yards from the bank then you could well catch fish. In the winter, or when the water is coloured, go for the smellier baits, such as meatballs or big hunks of luncheon meat.

🌅 **SEASON** – June 16th to March 14th.

🐟 **TICKETS** – you have to search along the Wye to find areas where you can barbel fish throughout the season between June 16th and March 14th. Some areas do allow you on when salmon fishing ends in October. There is excellent fishing in Hereford itself and double figure barbel are caught there most weeks. The fishing is controlled by the Hereford and District Angling Club and day tickets are priced at £3.50. Obtain these tickets at Woody's Tackle Shop in the town of Hereford, or phone 01432 344644. Woody is an expert on this stretch of the river and he will advise on other day ticket areas in and around the town. He also sells top quality maggots, so no need to bring your own. Moving upstream, you can also contact Richard Pennington on 01544 327294 at the famous Letton Court stretch. There are about one and a half miles of water here with some good pegs. The opposite bank is controlled by the Red Lion Hotel, where I have been giving barbel fishing courses now for

❧ STALKING CHUB ❧

The small, clear, overgrown rivers of central Wales in particular are often undiscovered havens for big chub. And I mean big! Catching them, though, can be another business and stalking individuals can often prove highly effective and thrilling.

- *Travel as light as possible. You don't want to tote unnecessary gear long distances along pretty well untended bankside.*
- *Rod, reel, bait and bag of assorted items are all you're likely to need. Carry a trout-type landing net that you can hang from your waist.*
- *Polaroid glasses are essential for spotting individual fish.*
- *Look for chub anywhere there's cover – deeper water, overhanging branches, fallen tree trunks, heavy weed – the sort of places chub can hide and mount an ambush. Make sure your gear is reasonably heavy – bullying a big chub from its tree-root sanctuary can be a difficult job.*
- *Best baits are slugs, lobworms, breadflake and even small, dead fish like minnows. Big, bold baits attract a chub's attention.*
- *Try the floating crust technique for flushing chub out of hiding. Break up twenty or so pieces of floating crust and throw them into the flow, watching them carefully as they go downstream. Frequently you'll find that they are taken at a point fifty, a hundred or even two hundred yards from you. Move down carefully and you know where the fish will be.*
- *If you try for a chub and scare it, you can always go back later. Richard Walker used to say chub become secure again at about ten minutes to the pound! Double it, I guess, for these pressurised days!*

ten years. Most of the water is reserved for hotel residents or course members, but there is about a mile of day-ticket river available. Contact Mike Taylor on 01981 500303.

Most of the river upstream is protected but there is some fishing available in Hay town centre with a few barbel showing there. There are also reports of barbel way into Wales at Builth Wells. Contact Pete Smith at the Caer Beris Manor Hotel, on 01982 552601, for details of fish appearing on the Irfon, a major tributary, and for accommodation.

ACCOMMODATION – both the Caer Beris Manor Hotel, on 01982 552601, and the Red Lion Hotel in Bredwardine, on 01981 500303, are highly recommended.

LLANGORSE LAKE

I have no hesitation in including Llangorse in this guide because it's a water that has given me some fabulous days. I just love it. Primarily, this is because you just won't find a more beautiful water anywhere, situated in its own little valley just to the west of the Black Mountains. It is a large water and, as fishing is by boat, you do feel as though you can get away from the rest of the world. When the day is fine and the sun is out, you just look around and realise coarse fishing doesn't come any better.

There's a good head of coarse fish in Llangorse, bream, perch and roach particularly. I've never targeted the bream but I've frequently seen them, especially in the shallow water where they've been muddying the water up as they feed. My plan for them, if I were ever to attempt them, would be to moor up at around twenty yards range and fish a moderate to heavy waggler on the fringe of their activity. By catapulting very small balls of ground bait laced heavily with maggots and casters I'd expect to pick up fish.

But it's the pike that have always attracted me to Llangorse. If we go back to Fred Buller's classic book, Domesday Pike, we'll find that is Llangorse mentioned there. Once upon a time, there was a run of salmon through the lake and, undoubtedly, pike did grow more massive in those days on the runs of classic silver tourists! Today, presumably, roach, bream and perch are there main fodder and their sizes have scaled down accordingly. There are still big pike to be had, though. As for methods, well all methods work at Llangorse, but my own preference is to drift slowly, working the water with a lure until I make contact. I might then anchor up and put a dead bait out while I search the area a bit more thoroughly.

Major words of caution here. Llangorse is beloved by the Welsh pike angler. It's the jewel in the crown. Please remember this and make sure that every single pike you hook in Llangorse is returned in the pristine condition you caught it in. You must take an unhooking mat along with you in your boat. Make sure that you have strong enough forceps or long-nosed pliers. Don't tackle Llangorse unless you know that you're a confident and competent pike angler. It's simply not fair to raid a water as fragile as Llangorse and harm the fish stocks.

93

Preaching over! A lovely water, whatever you are fishing for, and even on wild weather days the atmosphere remains. Just half close your eyes, take yourself back a hundred years or so and think of the monsters that once swam beneath your boat.

☼ SEASON – the closed season is from 14th March for six weeks.

✦ TICKETS – tickets and boats can be obtained from Ray Davies, Lakeside Caravan and Camping Park, Llangorse Lake, Brecon, Powys LD3 7TR, on 01874 658226. It is heartily advised that you plan a trip to Llangorse well in advance and make sure that everything is in order.

→ DIRECTIONS – Llangorse can be found off the A40 from Brecon to Abergavenny, to the northeast. From Abergavenny, turn right at Bwlch onto the B4560 and you will see Llangorse signposted on the left.

⊨ ACCOMMODATION – there is caravanning and camping on site. Alternatively, contact the Tourist Information Centre at Hay-on-Wye on 01497 820144 or at Brecon on 01874 622485.

COARSE FISHING IN PEMBROKESHIRE

Pembrokeshire is primarily a game-fishing area, but that doesn't mean to say that the coarse angler on holiday or visiting the area doesn't have some possibilities. There's some lovely fishing available. It's generally stillwater stuff but nicely controlled and, in places, with a pleasant, wild feel. Pembrokeshire itself is a stunning holiday area, and it's nice to know that sport and relaxation can be combined.

Breaking the mould, I'm simply going to give a list of the waters available along with contact phone numbers. Enquire for more specific details, such as directions and accommodation, when booking tickets.

BOSHERSTON LILY PONDS

Situated near Stackpole in the south of Pembroke, this is a flooded limestone valley managed by the National Trust. There's some interesting wildlife, with the rumour of otters. The ponds here have good stocks of coarse fish and the tench fishing is considered excellent. There are also roach, perch and good pike. You've got to get your permit first and this is available from Ye Olde Worlde Caf , Bosherston (01646 661216) or the National Trust Office in Stackpole (01646 661359). Also contact the Pembroke and District Angling Club (01646 622712) as this excellent club also has the lease on nearby Decoy Pond, a thirteen-acre water with some permits available.

PENHOYLE FISHING PARK, PENALLY, TENBY, SA70 7RG (01824 8422550

There is some good coarse fishing here in a carefully planned lake landscape. The scenery around is beautiful and the parkland that has been planted is maturing into a wilderness.

**PREMIER COARSE FISHERIES, HOLGEN FARM, LLAWHADEN, NARBERTH
SA67 8DJ (01437 541285)**
This is a fishery managed by Ian Heaps himself. I've met Ian at many of the game
shows and he speaks very highly of the water, as well he might. As a former world-
champion match angler, he certainly has the experience. There are three lakes here and
they're all well stocked with good carp and especially tench. Strongly recommended.

ROADSIDE FARM, TEMPLETON, NARBERTH, DYFED SA67 8DA (01834 891283)
This is another appealing water that holds common carp, mirror carp, bream, roach
and crucians. It is well stocked and set in serene surroundings. Contact Mr D. Crowley
at Roadside Farm.

WEST ATHESTON COARSE FISHERY, VALLEY FARM, NARBERTH, SA67 8BT (01834 860387)
This is only a one-and-a-half-acre lake, but it is very well stocked indeed with carp,
tench, perch, bream and roach. There are also rumours of grass carp, which are a
personal favourite of mine. Try hooking one on a thistlehead and you'll know what I
mean! I may not have caught many grass carp, but I really did catch one on a
thistlehead, and I also caught one on a four-inch piece of reed. You'd hardly believe it
was possible until it happens to you!

HALF ROUND POND – SOUTH WALES

If you find yourself down in the Swansea area and you are looking for a spot of
very pleasant fishing indeed, you can't do better than Half Round. This is a
really good fishery, roughly in the shape of a horseshoe but divided by a
narrow promontory to create two adjacent waters. The fishery extends to nearly
three acres and is set in a valley bordered by trees. In fact, you would never
guess that you were slap in the middle of a modern trading estate! It's a perfect
venue for children, especially with a bailiff to keep a watchful eye and good,
sound banks.

The fishing can also be well worthwhile. We're not talking huge fish here – the carp
go to double figures, though, and the tench reach nearly five pounds. There are decent
perch and, in common with most Welsh waters, some big eels. Even better for children,
there are masses of tiny roach, always very willing biters on simple maggot. In fact,
simple baits are the order of the day. Bread, worm, maggot and sweetcorn are pretty
much all that you'll need. Floating baits are not allowed – sensible when you consider
the amount of waterfowl on the ponds – and nor are barbed hooks.

Half Round isn't going to provide you with the most earth-shattering fishing in the
world and you're not going to rewrite the record books but, considering its setting and
how close to urbanization it lies, it really does offer a breath of the countryside. And
above all, it's a tremendous stamping ground for children. Highly recommended.

☀ SEASON – open March 1st to February 12th.

✦ TICKETS – these cost £2.60 and the money is collected on the bank.

➔ DIRECTIONS – from junction 45 on the M4, follow the A4067 to Swansea. Turn left at the second exit. Turn right at the first roundabout and cross the second roundabout past Fendrod Lake. The ponds are behind the Wyevale garden centre at the next roundabout.

⊨ ACCOMMODATION – contact the Swansea Tourist Information Centre on 01792 468321 for details of various types of accommodation in this area.

DARREN LAKE – SOUTH WALES

An interesting lake, set close to the industrial areas of South Wales. In fact, the lake itself is on the site of a disused coal mine. There were two very deep lift shafts and these were left to overflow. As a result there now exist around four acres of very cold spring water, some four feet deep around the margins and plunging rapidly to a zone that is twenty to thirty feet deep – an interesting area of water to investigate when it is bakingly hot or achingly cold!

The stocks in the lake are good. There are big bream and tench nudging at least six pounds. The perch are reputed to be sensational. Locals say five pounds, but even if this is wishful thinking, you can still stake your hat on some big ones being present. There are also decent roach and rudd, some big eels and a few small pike that don't seem to attract much attention at all.

The carp fishing has potential. There are, almost certainly, fish to thirty pounds plus present. It's not an easy lake though, if only because it is situated in a park and there is a good deal of bankside disturbance. Also, you've got that extraordinary depth range to take into account. You've got other problems to contend with, too. For example, the fishing is only available during park opening times, so it's difficult to get away from the madding crowd at times.

Nevertheless, this is a fascinating lake and it serves the area very well. It's run by the Glyncornel Angling Association and they keep a very careful eye on the water. Note that barbless hooks are mandatory.

☀ SEASON – open March 1st to February 12th. It's only closed for a short time between February 13th and 28th/29th.

✦ TICKETS – day tickets cost £5, season tickets £20 for adults and £15 for children/ concessions. Contact Paul's Army and Navy Stores, Tonypandy, on 01443 432856, or David Piction-Davies on 01443 432289..

➔ DIRECTIONS – from the A465 at Hirwaun, take the A4059 to Aberdare. Follow the A4233 through Maerdy to Ferndale and turn right by the Rhondda Hotel. Darren Park is just past the school on the right.

⊨ ACCOMMODATION – the Tourist Information Centre in Pontypridd, on 01443 490748, will give advice on suitable accommodation.

The Ouse, even in flood, is an exciting river to fish. The size of its barbel is legendary, and the chub are not far behind. Perch, too, are coming through in numbers and size.

Blenheim Palace Lake offers some serious fishing opportunities. The tench, bream and pike fishing is unsurpassed in any other English estate lake.

Whenever you are fishing a river, try to get there at dawn. You'll find that most species feed well during this misty, magical period. Now is the time to go for barbel, chub and roach.

There's no wonder that barbel are the cult fish of the early twenty-first century. Large, cunning and hard-fighting, they're the species everyone wants at the end of their line.

To get the best out of a river you've really got to wade, providing, of course, the water is shallow and clear enough to do so in safety. Getting out in the current gives you greatly enhanced control.

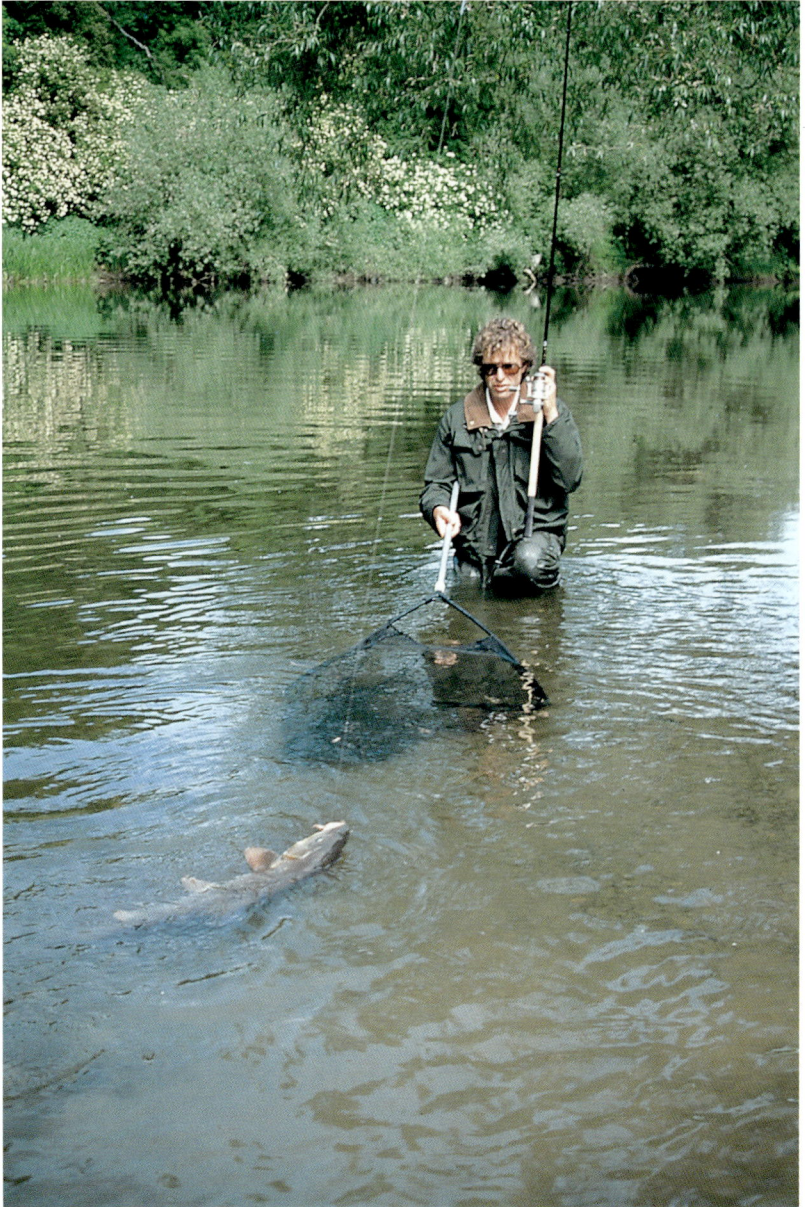

A nice barbel comes to the net. Take your time at this point, keep your rod well up, and always be prepared for a last, surging run. Set the clutch too tightly and a broken line could result.

- Nine Oaks, Oakford, Aberaeron, Cardiganshire. Plenty of good carp, roach, tench and bream in an area of Wales not overly blessed with good coarse waters. Phone 01545 580482 for details.
- Gowerton Carp Lake, Swansea. A good carp water close to the city situated on the Gowerton golf course. Plenty of carp including some good fish, averaging double figures. Fishes well in winter. Phone 01792 875188.
- Fendrod Lake, Swansea. This is situated in Swansea's Enterprise Park and is occasionally flooded by the adjacent River Tawe. This means that there are plenty of dace to be caught, along with the usual species. The contact number here is 01792 202245.
- Hazel Court, Cowbridge, South Glamorgan. Plenty of carp and some good rudd fishing. Also exotics like koi. Phone 01443 229601 for details.
- Riverside Maesycwmmer, Mid Glamorgan. A tremendous coarse lake with plenty of fish. Carp a target species but also roach and, notably, ide. Contact 02920 867513 for further details.
- Warren Mill, Nr. Cardiff. Excellent carp fishing and good roach in the winter. Also tench, bream and some big perch. Search out the deeper water along the dam. Phone 01446 781274.

COARSE-FISHING SITES IN THE NORTH

1. Longtown West Pond
2. The Lake District
3. Wyreside Lakes
4. Woodland Pool
5. Winsford Flash
6. Wall Pool Lodge
7. The River Swale
8. The River Ure
9. The River Ouse
10. Harthill Reservoirs

SCOTLAND

Berwick-upon-Tweed
Coldstream
Holy Island
Otterburn
NORTHUMBERLAND
Morpeth
Newbiggin-by-the-Sea
Ponteland
1 Longtown
Brampton
Carlisle
NEWCASTLE UPON TYNE
TYNE & WEAR
Washington
CUMBRIA
Penrith
Durham
Peterlee
Workington
DURHAM
Bishop Auckland
Hartlepool
Whitehaven
Brough
Stockton-on-Tees
Middlesbrough
Ambleside
Scotch Corner
Whitby
Lake District
2 Windermere
Kendal
Hawes
Northallerton
North York Moors
Scarborough
Ulverston
Kirkby Lonsdale
NORTH YORKSHIRE
Thirsk
Barrow-in-Furness
Morecambe
Lancaster
Ripon
8
Malton
Flamborough Head
Isle of Walney
Bridlington
Fleetwood
Skipton
Harrogate
9 York
EAST RIDING OF YORKSHIRE
LANCASHIRE
Keighley
Tadcaster
Market Weighton
Beverley
Blackpool
BRADFORD
LEEDS
Garforth
HULL
3 Preston
Burnley
W. YORKSHIRE
Blackburn
Goole
Southport
Rochdale
Huddersfield
Wakefield
Bolton
Barnsley
Thorne
Spur
Crosby
MANCHESTER
Doncaster
MERSEYSIDE
LIVERPOOL
Rotherham
SOUTH YORKSHIRE
Birkenhead
Warrington
SHEFFIELD
10
River Dee
Runcorn
Knutsford
Ellesmere Port
6
4 Chester
6 Middlewich
Macclesfield
Winsford
Congleton
Crewe
Nantwich
CHESHIRE

> ❛ *You know, for my job I travel all around the country, but I can never really wait to come back up north here, to my home. It's the wild waters, you see. All right, there is fishing pressure everywhere these days, but up here you can find stretches of river that you just know haven't been fished, at least not heavily, recently, if ever. And that reflects on the specimens themselves. Where else do you find chub so beautifully marked, in such cracking condition? There's plenty of variety too – enough to keep me going for a good few more years I'll tell you.* ❜

MARTIN JAMES

Martin James, the radio presenter, once explained to me why he left his native Kent and put down roots in the north. How right Martin is. Just look at the dazzling array of waters available. The Lake District is full of mystery. Windermere is beginning to open up as a really extraordinary pike water, and there are big, big perch in many of the other deep, clear lakes. My own best fish came from Bassenthwaite back in the 80s and what a beautiful fish it was. I was brought up on the lakes, canals, meres and rivers of Cheshire. In fact, I saw my first two-pound roach from the Peak Forest canal, a rural stretch just outside Macclesfield. I also saw my first big bream from Tatton Park, weighing in at six pounds and two ounces. Martin James himself is a dab hand on the River Ribble and has made real inroads into the chub, roach and barbel populations there.

Yorkshire, too, has a whole lot to offer. Rivers like the Swale, Ure and Nidd are spate waters, up and down like a fiddler's elbow and constantly asking questions of the angler. The barbel aren't colossal there, but they're fighting fit and live in large shoals, and there are great chub, super grayling and dace – in fact pretty well everything a river angler could want. And with the onset of commercial fisheries, there's now much more in the way of really big carp than there was just twenty or so years ago. In those days, you really had to sweat for a big fish, perhaps sitting for a season or more on a water like Redesmere .

THE NORTH

LONGTOWN WEST POND – CUMBRIA

I'm including this water because it's perched right in the north of the county, virtually on the borders with Scotland, and offers some excellent coarse fishing in an area that generally has little coarse fishing. West Pond is around twenty acres in extent, an old gravel pit going down to fifteen or sixteen feet in places. However, it's well matured and tree-lined, with a profusion of bars, plateaux and drop-offs. Also, most of the water isn't particularly deep and so is easily fished with a float. Partly because it is so shallow, it does get weedy in summer, and it might be an idea to take a drag, especially if you're fishing close in for the tench. There are good fish in the water. Carp reach twenty pounds, and bream have been recorded to double figures. The tench aren't very prolific but they are quite big, and the same goes for the perch. I'm also told there are some good stillwater chub in the water, genuinely reaching six pounds or so in weight.

All the usual pit techniques work here, and if you can find clear areas, especially at range, feed them up carefully with maggot, caster and corn. Swim feeder tactics also work well. Most carp, as expected, fall to boilies or, occasionally, luncheon meat.

Pike come to lures and dead baits – sardines are a favourite. (Please note that no live baiting is allowed on the water.) The chub are a different matter altogether. Stillwater chub virtually everywhere are very difficult beasts, and they're no different here. However, considering the sizes they run to, they are worth a bash. Try for them very early, at dawn, perhaps with a floater. Alternatively, go for dusk with perhaps a portion of dead fish. Do be careful of pike, though. Feed heavily with maggots in the hope of drawing chub into the area and getting them to intercept bait on the drop.

☀ SEASON – open all year.

🎣 TICKETS – these are £4.50 a day and it is best to phone in advance, on 01228 674519.

➡ DIRECTIONS – from Carlisle, take the A7 north to Longtown. Look for the A6071 signposted to Gretna. West Pond is at the bottom of the first turning on the left. The track leads to a car park.

🛏 ACCOMMODATION – for advice on suitable accommodation contact the Tourist Information Centre in Carlisle on 01228 625600.

THE LAKE DISTRICT – CUMBRIA

Anyone holidaying in the Windermere area with coarse fishing tackle in their car is in for a real treat. There is some really excellent coarse fishing within just a few miles of the town, invariably set in the most wonderful surroundings. You probably won't break national records, but that doesn't matter: the fish are fighting fit, in beautiful condition and there are backdrops to take your breath away. In large part, this access to such good fishing is a result of the splendid clubs in the area – most notably the Windermere, Ambleside and District

Angling Association. This worthy organization has several very good waters and offers day tickets to the visitor. You should try Ratherheath Tarn – a beautiful, tree-lined lake of about five acres in extent. Ratherheath offers tremendous tench fishing with individuals to about three or four pounds in weight. There are good bream, too, running well over five pounds and the carp are nudging their way into the upper doubles. There are also crucians, roach, rudd, chub and perch.

You don't have to fish too far out, and most people simply fish a waggler three to four lengths from the bank. Also, it pays to investigate marginal, snaggy areas. Try to get out to deeper water if you can – some of the longer platforms will take you to convenient drop-offs.

Ratherheath does attract the wind and this can make waggler fishing difficult. If it is windy, try either a straight lead or a small feeder, a method particularly favoured for the bream. All traditional baits work well, but maggots – especially red ones – and casters seem to pick up the bream. Small worms are also attractive to the bream, crucians and tench, and will occasionally attract a passing carp. All the traditional carp baits work well. In the very early morning, during warm weather, look for the carp in the shallows. They'll often come into water less than a foot deep and you'll see them feeding, throwing up mud clouds. Exciting stuff. A lobworm fished on a size six can often do the trick.

Holehird Tarn is another cracking WADAA water. It's an estate lake, dating back to the late 19th century. You have to buy tickets for Holehird before fishing. Only four day tickets are allowed, and this means that a serene day is pretty well guaranteed.

It's around three acres in extent and beautifully landscaped. It was made by damming a small stream, and this means that depths are about six feet at the dam to a mere foot or so near the inflow. There is plenty of bankside cover – lots of overhanging trees, along with lilies, weed beds and reeds.

There are some very good carp in Holehird, certainly reaching well into double figures. The crucian carp get to a pound or so and the tench are knocking five pounds. There are good roach, rudd and some pleasing bream.

Once again, look for the carp up in the shallows, especially early and late. You can get them on surface baits, but I'm told they are 'wising up'. Perhaps a bed of maggots will get them down or, once again, don't overlook that trusty lobworm.

Do make sure, however, that your tackle is up to the job. The carp fight very well indeed and they're rarely far away from snags. The association takes pride in the water and its fish stocks and it's only fair that you leave the place in as pristine a state as you find it.

The same goes for Grasmere. You just won't find a more beautiful water for pike anywhere in the British Isles. I promise you that. Weed can be something of a problem, especially in the summer. Grasmere is a prime tourist attraction so it often pays to get out early on the water, especially if you're fishing from the very accessible east bank.

Grasmere holds great stocks of perch and roach – both of which can reach a couple of pounds or so – but it's the pike that really make the fishery. Genuine thirty-pound fish have been caught and there are plenty of twenties every year. Smaller fish, just into doubles, are also prolific.

The fish come well to lures – try a surface lure, perhaps at dawn during settled weather conditions. Dead baits also do very well. (Please note that live baits are not allowed.) Try to vary your dead baits – eel sections are good, or even a lamprey or a small rainbow trout. Think carefully how you're going to present your dead bait. Make sure, for example, that you're not simply heaving it out into an extensive weed bed. Perhaps you can try one popped up with some polystyrene inserted in its throat?

Grasmere is the jewel in the crown of the WADAA so do take care of the pike stocks here. They are quite heavily fished and, although they may look ferocious with all those teeth, they are highly susceptible to bad handling. Always lay pike out on an unhooking mat – especially important if you're out in one of the rowing boats. Make sure that you have strong forceps or long-nosed pliers with you to get any deep hooks out. Ensure that you've flattened all the barbs on your trebles. If you are wary of going too near a pike's mouth, don't be afraid of wearing a good, stout, leather glove. When unhooking a pike, you've got to be confident. Don't dither. Lay the fish down, and if necessary, straggle it with your legs. If you've struck quickly and cleanly when dead baiting you should have the hooks close to the lips and they're much easier to remove here. Get that pike back into the water as quickly as possible. If you need a photograph, let it rest in the margins, in a net perhaps, while you set up the camera. Don't bother weighing every fish that comes along unless you think it's a personal best. Remember that every second out of the water causes these precious pike that extra bit of stress.

There's far more to the area than I've mentioned – Clea Barrow Tarn, Rydal Water, Blelham Tarn, Bassenthwaite, Coniston, Bigland Hall, the Ulverston Canal and so on. In fact, you can hardly do better than join the WADAA itself – you'll find this brings many benefits and the annual membership is very reasonable indeed.

SEASON – in general, often all year but check with the WADAA.

TICKETS – for Holehird, permits must be bought in advance. You can get them from Go Fishing, Robinson Place, Bowness on Windermere, Cumbria LA23 3DQ. Enclose a cheque and stamped addressed envelope. Day tickets cost £4 for adults and £2 for juniors. Phone 01539 447086 with enquiries. For Ratherheath, you can buy your permit at the Plantation Bridge Filling Station, which is just south of the fishery. For Grasmere – where day tickets are £3.50 – you can buy permits from the local Tourist Information Centres (of which there are many) or contact the WADAA direct. Contact Chris Sodo, Ecclerigg Court, Ecclerigg, Windermere, Cumbria LA23 1LQ on 01539 442708.

DIRECTIONS – from the mini roundabout on the A591 outside Windermere, take the A592 Ullswater road. Holehird Estate is on the right just after St. Anne's School for Girls, about half a mile from the roundabout. The fishery car park is clearly signed just inside the entrance to the estate. The Tarn is a short walk through the trees. To reach Ratherheath, go north on the A591 from the main Kendal roundabout. After half a mile the road becomes dual carriageway. A hundred and fifty yards into this section, turn left onto Ratherheath Lane. The fishery is on the right. Grasmere is found on the A591 north of Ambleside. You will come to it on the left, shortly after passing Rydal Water.

▬◄ ACCOMMODATION – all of the following can supply details of accommodation in their areas: Windermere Tourist Information Centre, Victoria Street, Windermere, on 01539 446499; Kendal Tourist Information Centre, Town Hall, Kendal, on 01539 725758; Ambleside Tourist Information Centre, Central Buildings, Market Cross, Ambleside, on 01539 432582.

⋙ LAKE PERCH ⋘

The Lake District in particular has had an outstanding reputation for large perch over the course of many years. These are fine, bristling fish, but how do you go about catching them?

• *Location is vitally important. You won't catch perch on large, deep waters unless you know where they are.*

• *Ask around and get as much local knowledge as you can. Trout fishermen are often particularly approachable. Perch don't mean too much to them!*

• *If you can, get afloat and take a fish finder with you. Remember that perch are shoal fish and they will frequently show up on the screen. Failing that, be as mobile as possible until you find fish. Explore by both bank and boat fishing as much acreage as you can. A good way to do this is to use lures. Perch like small spinners – especially with red wool around the tail. Try bright silvery plugs as well. Use Polaroid glasses and watch your lure as it comes into the bank. Perch will often follow without actually taking.*

• *Try trolling for perch – that is pulling small lures behind a moving boat. This way you're covering a lot of water rapidly and if you do contact perch, anchor up and fish the area carefully.*

• *Remember that top perch baits are small dead baits – minnows, gudgeon and the like, and also lobworms. One or two lobworms on a size four hook are difficult to beat.*

• *Try and get out a t dawn if you possibly can. This is a prime perch feeding time and you might well see perch on the prowl, chasing small fry around the margins or even bow waving after their own baby brethren. Remember that perch are very cannibalistic and a four inch dead perch is hard to beat for a grandmother.*

• *Perch are particularly susceptible to stress. Don't keep them in a net but photograph them and, if necessary, weigh them and return them as quickly as possible.*

WYRESIDE LAKES – LANCASHIRE

Sometimes commercial fisheries really do hit the jackpot and offer fishing that is way beyond anything that so-called natural waters can produce. This is certainly the case at Wyreside. The Wyreside complex, just off the River Wyre, holds seven waters, each offering vastly different challenges. The predominant theme, however, is carp fishing. There is a staggering number of big fish in the lakes – carp reaching almost forty pounds, very large indeed for the north.

However, you don't have to leap in big-time. This is what makes it such a perfect place for a holidaying angler, perhaps with children who want to know the ropes. Tuition, by the way, is also available. It's generally considered by the regulars that Foxes Lake is the best place for the general angler. There are carp there in numbers and size, but they're not too desperately difficult to catch. Moreover, there are big tench, lots of bream, huge stocks of roach and rudd along with perch, crucians and chub in this very prolific four-acre water.

There are well-known hotspots – the outflow pipes especially – but fishing a feeder at range is generally considered one of the surest ways of building up a bag. Hemp is considered an important base to fishing at Foxes and is available on site if you can't bring yourself to cook your own! Maggots, sweetcorn and worms all work well also.

Foxes is a favourite venue so, as on all comparatively pressurised waters, it doesn't pay to be stereotypical. Try something just a little bit unconventional and you could get a surprise. Why not, for example, mix casters in with your feed and then try ten or eleven of them squeezed onto a size six or eight hook.

There are other lakes all the way up the ladder of difficulty. Sunnyside One holds plenty of better-sized carp and is considered the next step to take. At the top of the pyramid is Wyre Lake, a real big-fish water, holding several carp over thirty pounds.

A really great complex, attractive to look at, very welcoming, with great fish stocks, and altogether highly recommended.

SEASON – open all year.

TICKETS – there is a whole scale of charges depending on which lake you are fishing and how long you are at the waterside. For Foxes – the most popular family choice – a full day costs from as little as £4.50. There's also a children's lake where under-twelves fish free if they have a parent on the fishery. Phone Wyreside Lakes on 01524 792093 for full details.

DIRECTIONS – take the M6 northwards from Preston. At Junction 33, just after the Lancaster Service Station, turn left at the first roundabout, and then immediately left onto Hampson Lane. At the end of the lane turn right (you will see the signs to the fishery). Go past the Fleeced Inn pub and then right and left and you will come to the waters.

ACCOMMODATION – there is camping on site. Details of other accommodation can be obtained from the Tourist Information Centre in Lancaster on 01524 32878. The fishery is also reasonably close to Morecambe, where there is a host of various kinds of accommodation. Phone the Tourist Information Centre there on 01524 582808.

WOODLAND POOL – SOUTH WIRRAL

There are four lakes at this day ticket venue but this is probably the most beautiful. All the lakes are mature and they have become hugely popular in the area. There are islands, weed beds, reed margins and lots of overhanging trees – a real gem of a pool.

Fish stocks are generous. The crucian fishing is excellent and you tend to find these in the margins, especially under the weeds and in the tree roots. The tench – some of them very good fish indeed – tend to hang around the islands, and the carp are absolutely suckers for floating baits when the temperatures are reasonably stable. Mind you, they can be infuriatingly fussy. Make sure that your line immediately preceding the hook bait is under the surface, because if they see it in the surface film you are unlikely to get a bite. There are even a few catfish in the lake and chub have recently been introduced. Please note that keep nets are not allowed – another sign of pride in a fishery.

☀ SEASON – open all year.

⚓ TICKETS – day tickets cost £6 for one rod. Night fishing costs £10. Phone 0151 353 0115 for further details.

➡ DIRECTIONS – from Chester, take the A540 northwest toward Hoylake. After the junction with the A550, take the third turning on the left signposted Burton. The fishery is well signposted in the village.

🛏 ACCOMMODATION – contact the Tourist Information Centres in Birkenhead, on 0151 647 6780, and/or Chester, on 01244 402111, for details of accommodation in the area.

WINSFORD FLASH – CHESHIRE

This is a spacious, seventy-acre flash that is fed by the River Weaver. Forty-five acres of the water are available on day permit. Depths average around about six feet but there are deeper pockets, especially out in the middle, which reach twelve and thirteen feet. The fish stocks, though, are excellent. Carp are a big draw with lots of doubles and big fish approaching thirty. The water is full of bream, which are not generally large, but there are rumours of double-figure fish here. There are many pike and numerous doubles, along with tench, big perch and two pound roach.

Both pole and waggler approaches work well, but if you really want to get into the bream, the ground bait feeder attack is probably the best. Remember that the bream stocks really are prolific and this isn't the sort of water where you build up a big bag with just half a pint of maggots or so. Keep the feed going in but, as always with bream fishing, beware of putting big balls directly above a feeding shoal's head. Bites can get a bit twitchy as water temperatures drop later in the year and this is where sensitive indication and the very best quality bait begins to pay off. A single caster on a size sixteen hook, along with a small redworm, has long been one of my own personal favourites for temperamental bream. Waters like this are a lot of fun: when your float goes down you simply don't have a clue what species could be next to come to your waiting net.

⚓ **SEASON** – open all year.

🎣 **TICKETS** – these cost £3 per day and are available down on the bankside. Junior tickets are £1.50. Night tickets are £5 and £2.50. Phone 01606 558475.

➡ **DIRECTIONS** – on the A54 from Middlewich to Winsford, you will come to the central Winsford roundabout. This crosses the River Weaver. Continue up the hill and at the second set of traffic lights turn left along Dene Drive. Turn left at the first roundabout into Queensway and on into Ways Green. You will see signs now for Winsford Flash. You come to the dirt road and turn right before the caravan park. The Flash is on your left and parking is ample. Do note, however, that certain areas of the Flash are out of bounds.

🛏 **ACCOMMODATION** – there is bed and breakfast accommodation very close to the site. Phone 01606 592186, or contact the Tourist Information Centre in Nantwich, on 01270 610983, who can supply details of further accommodation in the area.

❧ CHOOSING SWIMS ON BIG WATERS ❧

Huge reservoirs and gravel pits can be intimidating places to fish simply because the location is so daunting.

- *Fish of most species tend to follow the wind. Most winds in this country blow from the south and west so banks to the north and east are generally favourite.*
- *Look for any possible features, islands, bays, shallow bars, water towers, inflowing streams. Fish might not necessarily be around these features but they do give you a starting point.*
- *Look intently for signs of surface activity. You might see a crashing carp, or the backs of rolling bream.*
- *Binoculars are a great help when looking for fish.*
- *On a windy day you will sometimes see a large flat area of water appear. This is a sign of a big fish turning underneath.*
- *Remember that even on the largest of waters fish aren't necessarily always out on the horizon but can be close in to the margins.*
- *If you are pike fishing, a drift float rig can get your dead baits one hundred and fifty yards or more out from the bank. A great method.*
- *Don't be afraid to ask bailiffs for any information they might be able to give. It is their job to make sure you're a happy fisherman!*

WALL POOL LODGE – CHESHIRE

Gawsworth is the most gorgeous of rural villages, set deep in the Cheshire countryside, and the lakes there, when I was a child, were always something of a dream for me. This is real, sleepy, rural fishing. Wall Pool Lodge offers three well-stocked and very beautiful woodland pools. They're exactly as I remember from childhood, girt by rushes and ornamented by lily pads.

Wood Pool is probably the largest of the waters, followed by Park Pool and Wall Pool, and they are all well stocked. Wall Pool, however, has a real reputation for ghost carp. These beautiful and shy fish average about five pounds. There are also good tench, roach and rudd. All the lakes hold big crucians and interesting perch. There are carp to approaching twenty pounds and good bream.

Despite the number of fish, they're not always that easily caught – it pays to fish close to features and to get to the water early.

 SEASON – open all year.
 TICKETS – these cost £5. They are best pre-booked, on 01260 223442.
 DIRECTIONS – Gawsworth is just outside Macclesfield on the A536 Congleton Road. In the village, follow the signs to Gawsworth Hall. Go through the gate and the fishery is well signposted.
 ACCOMMODATION – advice on various types of accommodation in the area can be obtained from the Tourist Information Centres in Macclesfield, on 01625 504114, and Buxton, on 01298 25106.

THE RIVER SWALE – YORKSHIRE

Go back thirty years or so and the River Swale was the barbel Mecca of the north. In fact, my first trips after the species were spent at the then very famous Topcliffe stretch. I was never successful myself, though nearly... One glorious morning I actually hooked what was obviously a barbel. It tore off against a clutch that couldn't have been screwed down more tightly with a pair of pliers. There wasn't much stretch in the nylon lines of old and the result was simply inevitable. I received a justified ticking off from the adult club members that I've never forgotten.

It is a fact that too many barbel are lost, especially by those that haven't had a great deal of experience fishing for them. Always make sure YOUR CLUTCH is set properly and can give line if it has to, your knots are secure, your hook point is sharp and that you're not going too light on the breaking strain.

Also, watch out for that famed last rush, because it is a fact. Well over ninety percent of barbel will make another strong, spirited run when they see the landing net. Be ready, and have your rod up and your clutch set lightly so that you're not going to leave a hook in a tired fish.

The Swale has always responded well to maggots and casters – and you'll pick chub, grayling and roach on these. In some stretches, bream have also been stocked, and these are beginning to grow and to spread. Don't neglect the usual baits: meatballs work well, and if the water is high and coloured, try two or even three on a big hook.

SEASON – phone 01609 776850 to check on the current situation.

TICKETS – an excellent stretch can be found at Morton-on-Swale. Day tickets cost £5 and must be obtained from Morton Service Station before fishing. You'll find this at the river end of this small village. In case of problems, phone 01609 776850. Obviously, if you are contemplating an early start, get your ticket the day before.

DIRECTIONS – turn off the A1, south of Scotch Corner onto the A684. You'll be heading eastwards towards Northallerton. In about three or four miles, you will come to Morton Bridge where there is good parking in the lay-by adjacent. The river can be reached along the paths at the bridge, at Swalefields Farm or Fairholme Farm. These are all situated down the lane on the right after passing over the bridge. Morton village will be just in front of you.

ACCOMMODATION – advice on various kinds of accommodation can be obtained from the Tourist Information Centre in Northallerton, on 01609 776864.

THE RIVER URE – YORKSHIRE

I have the happiest memories of the Ure, this sparkling Yorkshire river. Find the right stretches and you'll be in a wonderland. Nice, eddying deeps, glistening shallows and enticing, steady glides. And, generally, flowing through stunning countryside. What can you expect on the Ure? Well, barbel certainly. These might not run as large as in some of the southern rivers, but they're cracking fish nonetheless and fight spectacularly. You can catch them in all sorts of ways but, if you can, try and get out early in the morning and stalk them in the shallows. They come from the deeps during the night to feed on caddis, loach, leeches, anything they can find in and around those gravely margins. Approach them really cautiously – you'll often see their fins on bow waves – and free-line a single lobworm just upstream of them. Watch that line streak tight!

You'll find grayling, too, and what's better than float fishing for them on a crisp, autumn morning? And, of course, like all the Yorkshire rivers, the Ure is famous for its chub. These can grow large, but be satisfied with any fish over a couple of pounds or so. Of course, chub will come on maggots and casters, but never neglect a really big lump of flake. And I mean big. A piece the size of an orange will often overcome the suspicions of chub that are used to light gear and small baits. In short, summer or winter, a brilliant river.

SEASON – at present, rivers still have a closed season but a change is threatened. Check on your ticket for the latest details.

TICKETS – there are several places where day ticket access is available. Ripon is a good place to start and Ripon Piscatorial Association sells day tickets for £4. A useful contact here is Bernard Thain at the Ripon Angling Centre, on 01765 604666. There are also day tickets available on the Newby Hall Estate at Boroughbridge. Phone the tackle shop Fish-n-Things on 01423 324776. Day tickets cost £4.50.

DIRECTIONS – for the Ripon stretch, take the A61 or B6265 east to access points. You will see the parking areas shown on your ticket. Fish-n-Things (see above) will give detailed instructions on purchase of ticket.

ACCOMMODATION – the Tourist Information Centre in Ripon, on 01765 604625, can give advice on suitable accommodation.

THE RIVER OUSE – YORKSHIRE

I've never done nearly as well on the Ouse as I feel I should have done and in part this is because it is bigger, deeper and less easy to read, I guess. Still, it does have very good fish in it. You'll find roach, bream, perch, chub, barbel and good pike in most stretches of the river. Perch can grow large and the barbel, though not that easy to contact, can be huge.

There's some excellent free fishing just northwest of York itself. So, if you are visiting this wonderful, ancient town it is worth putting a selection of gear into the car. The pole works very well here, as do both waggler and stick floats. Probably favourite, however, is feeder with maggot. Good bags are possible, especially if you get out of the city early in the morning and catch that early feeding spell.

SEASON – phone 01904 654484 to check on current situation

TICKETS – these are free, but the nearest tackle shop, Mitre Pets, Shipton Road, York, will give further details. You can contact them on 01904 654484.

DIRECTIONS – from York, take the A19 road to Thirsk. In a very short while you will come to a road on the left called Waterend. Park in the lay-by on the left, just before the bridge.

ACCOMMODATION – contact the Tourist Information Centre in York on 01904 621756. They can give details of various kinds of accommodation in the area.

HARTHILL RESERVOIRS – SOUTH YORKSHIRE

I've never actually fished Harthill, but a couple of visits there without tackle have impressed me immensely. There's something noble about these reservoirs so close to the city of Sheffield. Number One reservoir is large and deep, especially by the main dam where, with depths approaching thirty feet, you can catch roach in the coldest of winter weather. The opposite end of the reservoir is shallower with a deep channel running through it. There are all sorts of fish here to be caught, often good-sized ones. The carp and pike both pass twenty pounds and

109

there are reputedly double figure bream and tench approaching that mark. There are good roach, as well, in the reservoirs – some say two-pound fish.

Number Two reservoir is both smaller and shallower than Number One, but it nonetheless offers some good sport, especially with carp. Reservoir Number Three is the shallowest of them all.

The local anglers fish the water intently. Hemp, ground bait with casters and redworms seem favourite for roach and bream. Occasionally, try just turning the reel handle a couple of times so that the hook bait inches back along the reservoir bed. All manner of carp baits seem to do the trick, but for pike you've got to think of presenting a dead bait in an untypical fashion if you're going to get the best out of the water. They've simply seen too many dead herrings presented hard on the bottom. Perhaps you could use a drifter float, moving a sardine slowly through the mid-water regions. Or go for a more exotic dead bait – really search your tackle dealer's freezer or the local fishmonger. And don't forget eel sections – tremendously effective. I've also got a feeling that very small flat fish could prove interesting!

☀ SEASON – open all year.

✠ TICKETS – these are available on the water. They cost £3 for a day and £6 for a night. Phone 01142 207352 for details. There are many concessions.

➡ DIRECTIONS – take the A618 south from Rotherham. Just before you reach the M1, turn off left towards Woodall and Harthill. Turn onto Carver Close and you will find parking by the first reservoir.

🛏 ACCOMMODATION – the Tourist Information Centre in Sheffield, on 01142 211900, can advise on suitable accommodation.

- *Pebley Reservoir, Harthill, South Yorkshire. At around twenty-five acres, Pebley is a large water and very picturesque, nestling in its wooded valley. Big tench and bream, including roach around the two-pound mark. There are some big pike and good perch. The carp now are plentiful. Contact Dave Downes on 0966 361005.*
- *The River Swale at Cundall Lodge Farm, Boroughbridge, Yorkshire. A tremendous piece of the river, offering very good chub fishing. There are also good numbers of barbel, roach and perch. Worm is seen as a good bait, along with the usual luncheon meat. Day tickets cost £3 and you pay in the farmyard. Contact Fish 'n' Things, Boroughbridge. Phone them on 01423 324776 for bait and up to the minute advice on conditions.*
- *Tyram Hall Fishery, Hatfield, South Yorkshire. Four pools available. Some big carp, plenty of doubles, and the main lake holds good numbers of roach, bream and tench. Also some good pike and fish approaching twenty-five pounds have been landed. A good all-round fishery. Tickets cost between £3 and £6. Phone Phil Johnson on 01302 840886.*
- *The River Don, Doncaster, South Yorkshire. Not the most elegant of fisheries, but worth trying as it's pretty well come back from the dead. Today there are good roach, perch, chub and even the occasional barbel. Day tickets cost £2.50. Contact Doncaster Match Secretary, Lee Granta, on 01302 781016 for further details and directions.*
- *Flylands Pond, Bishop Auckland, County Durham. A small two-acre pond with a central island and depths to around four or five feet. Small carp, tench and skimmers but some good roach. Plenty of fish. Good for beginners. Tickets are £5 a day on the bank. Contact 01388 832362.*
- *Fir Tree Lodges, Appley Bridge, Wigan, Lancashire. Two lakes here. Nicely matured. Carp to mid twenties, big tench and chub. Reputed three-pound roach and perch and some good crucians. Also some golden and blue orfe. Lots of fish, lots of potential surprises. Tickets £5 a day on the bank. Phone 01257 252607 for further details.*
- *Borwick Fishery, Carnforth, Lancashire. A ten-acre gravel pit holding big carp and bream plus good tench, roach and perch. Not a particularly easy water but the rewards are impressive for the specialist angler. This is a popular fishery, so check on availability and ticket prices by phoning 01254 720844.*

Coarse-Fishing Sites in Scotland

1. River Tweed
2. Barend Loch
3. Oauchenreoch Loch
4. Duddingston Loch
5. Clatto Country Park
6. Glasgow Fishing
7. Loch Lomond
8. Loch Awe
9. Loch Garry
10. Loch Ness
11. River Tummel

Shetland Islands

Lerwick

Orkney Islands

WESTERN ISLES

Duncansby Head

Thurso

Noss Head

Wick

Uig

Isle of Skye

Tain

Tarbat Ness

HIGHLAND

Alness

Dingwall

Inverness

Nairn

Forres

Elgin

Banff

Fraserburgh

MORAY

Peterhead

A9

A96

A98

Canna

Rum

Loch Ness

Aberdeen

Stonehaven

Fort William

Coll

Tiree

Pitlochry

Ballinluig

Blairgowrie

Brechin

Montrose

Forfar

Arbroath

Isle of Mull

Oban

Dalmally

Crianlarich

Dundee

Crieff

Perth

St Andrews

FIFE

Fife Ness

Colonsay

ARGYLL AND BUTE

Tarbet

Stirling

Kinross

Jura

Greenock

Clydebank

Dunfermline

Kirkcaldy

EDINBURGH

Dunbar

Islay

GLASGOW

Hamilton

Eyemouth

Ardrossan

Strathaven

Bigger

Galashiels

Coldstream

Arran

Kilmarnock

Lesmahagow

Selkirk

Campbeltown

Ayr

Cumnock

Hawick

Jedburgh

Mull of Kintyre

Girvan

Moffat

Lockerbie

Langholm

Newton Stewart

Dumfries

Castle Douglas

Stranraer

Dalbeattie

Sandy Hills

Luce Bay

DUMFRIES AND GALLOWAY

N

' *For the man who really wants a bit of adventure, my guess is you can't do better than coarse fishing in Scotland. The point is there are just no signposts up here. Everything is fresh and new, and most things you've got to find out for yourself. I've been coming up to Scotland for around fifteen years – mostly with pike gear – and there's still hardly anything I do know, never mind things I don't. Mind you, you will catch fish, Probably! What is definite is that you will never catch pike that look better and fight more magnificently. They really are tigers. Unbelievable. There's more, obviously. The perch can grow big here, and in the lowland belt you've got some very interesting roach and dace fishing for instance. But, for me, it's the Highlands every time.* '

ROGER MILLER —ANGLING AUTHOR

Roger is absolutely spot on with this assessment of Scottish fishing. The lowland belt does offer more conventional delights. Here you can catch bream, roach, dace, tench and carp, but it is as you climb north that the real lure of Scotland begins to grab you.

The lochs are vast, largely uncharted, bodies of water and it's only really Loch Lomond that anybody knows a great deal about. Trek further than that and you are beginning to break some new territory. But don't be too worried – you're not totally on your own. There have been enlightened fishermen for many years who have understood what piking in the north of Scotland is all about and have appreciated its possible, awe-inspiring boundaries.

Who can actually tell how big Scottish pike can actually grow? We know, of course, that twenties and thirties are to be caught. Nor do I have any doubt that there are forty-pounders in some lakes. And fifties? Well, rumours abound that pike of that sort of size were taken back in the last century, either on rod and line or in nets laid out to rid trout waters of them.

RIVER TWEED – SCOTTISH BORDERS

Naturally enough, whenever an angler thinks of the Tweed it's salmon that pulls his imagination. However, for the touring coarse fisherman, a lot more is on offer. It was back in the 1960s that the huge roach of the River Tweed really began to make ripples in the angling world. Roach of two pounds were common. Three-pounders were anything but rare. Dace of a pound littered the river. More and more anglers, especially from northern England, began to make their way to the Tweed, and huge catches were taken.

And so it was through the 70s, before catches began to decline somewhat in the early 80s. Now, there is a rumour that roach and dace are on their way back in both numbers and size. I'm not necessarily saying that the fishing you'll find on the Tweed is going to be easy. It certainly will be, though, if you search enough water and find the fish. Believe me, the roach shoals can be large and obliging. The key is to keep on the move, watch for any surface activity and, above all, take local advice.

If you can keep them fresh, swim feeder maggots can work very well where allowed, although bread and worms also take their fair share of fish. My own best bag was built up in Coldstream, just by the bridge on the crease of a huge slack a third of the way across the river. If I remember correctly, in a four-hour session I took some thirty roach over a pound, with two of them going over two pounds to just on two pounds and four ounces. Intermingled were some twenty or thirty fine dace.

I've included this entry because the rewards can be great for the angler willing to risk a slow day or two. But, of course, a day on the Tweed is never wasted. This majestic river in such wondrous countryside is a water to be loved no matter what the day's results might bring.

SEASON – there is no close season for coarse fish in Scotland, although it pays to check on local rules that may protect areas of water when migratory fish are spawning. Ring the secretary of Coldstream and District Angling Association, M. Young Esq., on 01573 226411 for up-to-the-minute information. He can also advise on day tickets for brown trout and grayling.

TICKETS – tickets can be bought for £2 a day from the Crown Hotel in Market Square, on 01890 882558, and from the Coldstream Guardian, on 01890 883164. The Norhambridge area is well worth a look for roach, perch and dace, and tickets can be bought for £4 a day from the Masons Arms, the Victoria Hotel, the Mace Shop and the Shepherd Shop all in Norham village itself. Kelso is also a centre for coarse fishing. Tickets for £4 a day can be bought from: Forest and Sons, 40 The Square; Intersport, 43 The Square; and Tweedside Tackle, 36–38 Bridge Street – all in Kelso.

ACCOMMODATION – a huge amount of bed and breakfast accommodation is available in the area along with some exceptional hotels. The Tillmouth Park Hotel, on 01890 882255, is quite spectacular and offers some excellent fishing of its own. In Kelso, try the Cross Keys Hotel on 01572 223303, or the Ednam House Hotel, which is right on the River Tweed itself, on 01573 223303.

BAREND LOCH – DUMFRIES AND GALLOWAY

Barend is one of those rare beasts up in Scotland – a carp-only fishery. It used to be trout but competition forced a change of use for the water, so the trout were taken out and the carp put in. Most of them are either ghost carp or commons, which makes for an interesting mix. The fish aren't yet of a huge size, but they're in good condition, there are plenty of them and they fight well in the clear water. Barend extends to around three acres. It's picturesque and surrounded by trees, and an island adds some focus. The lake is man-made but it is spring-fed and that accounts for its clarity. Most of the water is quite shallow, but there are areas that go down to nine or ten feet.

The pool can be approached in a variety of ways. For smaller carp, close-in float fishing with corn, scraps of meat and maggots, for example, works well. Try laying on or fishing just on the bottom under a waggler. For larger carp, look for the deeper water and try ledgering larger baits. Luncheon meat, again, works well as, obviously, do all manner of boilies.

Don't neglect floaters either. Dog biscuits and bread crust both work well, especially on warmer days when fishing on or near the bottom can be difficult. Ideal conditions, overall, are warm, wet, windy days when light values are low.

Barend is all part of a holiday village complex, so it's an ideal place to take the family, get away from everything, explore the lowlands and do a bit of carp fishing in the evening before or after supper.

☼ SEASON – open all year.

⚡ TICKETS – day tickets cost £5 and are available from the holiday complex reception. Buy these before fishing. Contact Frank Gorley, Barend Loch, Sandy Hills, Dumfries and Galloway, Scotland, on 01387 780663.

➡ DIRECTIONS – take the A710 from Dumfries towards Sandy Hills. Turn right onto the road signposted to Dalbeattie and you'll find the fishery shortly on the left. The holiday complex reception, which you must visit, is on the right.

⊨ ACCOMMODATION – either stay on site or contact the Dumfries and Galloway Tourist Board on 01387 245550.

OAUCHENREOCH LOCH – DUMFRIES AND GALLOWAY

This very picturesque loch, lying very close to the A75, offers some spectacular perch and pike fishing. It's a natural loch, long and narrow, averaging around fifteen feet. It does go deeper – reputedly to fifty feet – and the water is generally clear. It also gets weedy, which goes a long way to explaining why the perch stocks are so good. You can target them successfully when the weed dies off from October onwards.

There are several ways of approaching the water and for the small roach and small perch that proliferate, simply float fishing with maggots does well. For larger perch, try either lure fishing or drifting a dead bait. Should a small perch accidentally die through deep hooking, for example, you cannot find a better bait. If it is taken, don't delay too long in striking, as a two-pound perch can quickly gobble down one of its smaller brethren. I aim for about four or five seconds before striking with a slow deliberate sweep.

The pike average a good size and have been caught to mid twenties with plenty of rumours of the odd thirty-pounder being seen. Once again, perch is a good dead bait for them but in this clear water lure fishing always works well. One last tip: if you are fishing a dead bait for perch, always make sure that you use a wire trace in case a pike picks up the bait.

Boats are allowed on the loch, which gives you more scope to explore unfishable water. Bank fishing is only available on the road side of the water.

☀ SEASON – all year round.

✔ TICKETS – these costs £3 and are obtained at the Loch View Motel before fishing. Phone 01556 690281

➜ DIRECTIONS – the loch lies between Dumfries and Castle Loch by the side of the main A75. Leave Dumfries heading towards Castle Douglas and you'll find the fishery on the right-hand side a little way through Crocketford.

🛏 ACCOMMODATION – the Loch View Motel is right on the water. Advice on other accommodation can be obtained from the Dumfries and Galloway Tourist Board, 64 Whitesands, Dumfries DG1 2RS, or phone 01387 245550.

DUDDINGSTON LOCH – EDINBURGH

How about this! Duddingston is a twenty-five acre loch set in the scenic grounds of Holyrood Park – owned by the Queen herself – and the fishing is free! It's basically a nature reserve and bird sanctuary, but you are still allowed free access to a hundred-yard stretch of the banks. You won't find much depth – in no place is the loch much deeper than six or seven feet – but you will find good fish. The primary species are roach, perch and carp that grow respectively to two, three and twenty-plus pounds. Ledgering further out is the best bet for the carp, but closer-in float-fishing tactics with maggots do well for the roach and perch. Alternatively, try a bunch of lobworms for a bigger perch or even a small dead sprat.

The rumours were that cormorant attacks had reduced the stocks somewhat, but fishing once again seems to be very well worthwhile and offers a real bonus so close to the centre of this great capital city.

☀ SEASON – open all year round.

⚓ TICKETS – the tickets are free but a permit to fish must be obtained from the park gates at Holyrood Park. Contact Mike Heath on 0131 657 3258. Under no circumstances leave litter, use keep nets or try to fish on after dark. And it is much appreciated if you do pick up any litter you should happen to chance upon. Remember that anglers are very much in the public eye in this sensitive area.

➡ DIRECTIONS – head south into Edinburgh on the A1 and turn off left to Duddingston village. Follow the road past the church, and park in the car park opposite the loch itself. It's easily found.

🛏 ACCOMMODATION – the Edinburgh and Lothian Tourist Board, Edinburgh and Scotland Information Centre, 3 Princes Street, Edinburgh EH2 2QP can supply information about accommodation in the area on 0131 473 3800.

✦ LURE FISHING TIPS ✦

If you fish with multiplier reels, be very careful not to let them fall on sand or grit, as a single particle in the mechanism can destroy the smooth running of the reel and make casting very difficult. Remember when casting to use a progressive pendulum-type movement.

- *WD40 is perfect for getting a reel to run smoothly again. Spray the reel and allow half an hour or so for the oil to penetrate. Then wipe off the surplus.*
- *Look after your lures. Keep them neatly stocked away and use bonnets to mask the hook points, or you will get into terrible tangles.*
- *Keep big spoons and spinners well polished. A shiny lure reflects the light much more efficiently than a tarnished one.*
- *Try painting white blotches on a large plug with Tippex or a marker pen. A predator recognises white on a prey fish as fungus and a sick fish means an easy meal.*
- *Braid line is now an accepted part of the lure fisher's armoury – make sure, however, that you tie the right knots!*
- *Even if you are lure fishing for perch, always use a wire trace, as a pike can easily take a spinner not intended for it!*
- *Don't restrict yourself to plugs, spoons and spinners. Open your mind to jerk baits and especially jigs – rubber imitations of fish, frogs, lizards and so on. Jig fishing is great fun and highly effective.*
- *If you need lures, don't forget that the Harris Angling Company, on 01692 581208, are the country's leading lure experts and can mail anything to you within 24 hours wherever you are in the UK.*

CLATTO COUNTRY PARK – DUNDEE

Clatto is a former reservoir, around twenty-five acres in extent. It averages around ten feet and drops down to twenty feet plus. It is set now in a country park and so anglers are very much on view.

Only half the lake is actually open to anglers, so do make sure that you don't stray past the limits – the rangers office is close by, and you won't be fishing there for long!

The large amounts of smaller perch and roach are the main attraction of the water, but there are some real specimen perch lurking in the water – possibly topping the three-pound mark. There are also some very good tench and bream – reaching six or seven pounds – and carp are also occasionally taken. Do make sure that you obey the fishery rules here because they are strict – no live baiting and no spinning.

☀ **SEASON** – open all year.

✹ **TICKETS** – these cost £1.80. Phone 01382 435911 in advance.

➡ **DIRECTIONS** – from the A90 Perth to Dundee, turn off onto the A923 on the outskirts of Dundee. This is signposted Angus Coupar. You will see signs for Clatto Country Park in approximately one mile.

◻ **ACCOMMODATION** – information about various kinds of accommodation available in the area can be obtained from the Angus and Dundee Tourist Board, 21 Castle Street, Dundee DD1 3AA, on 01382 527527.

COARSE FISHING IN THE GLASGOW AREA

Glasgow is, today, a vibrant bustling city unmissable if you're into the arts, culture or simply shopping! It's a perfect holiday destination for a few days, and it's well worthwhile putting some coarse-fishing tackle into the back of the car. Of course, when you think of Scotland you tend to think of salmon and trout, but the Glasgow area has a lot more to offer. The Clyde itself has some cracking grayling fishing available, and in some parts offers free fishing. You also have the Forth and Clyde canal with good pike, perch, roach, tench, rudd and bream. There is no close season on the canal, and day tickets are just £1. For further details apply to British Waterways, 1 Applecross Street, Glasgow GP4 9SP, on 0141 3326936.

There's also plenty of free fishing in and around Glasgow city centre. You could try Uchenstarry Pond for tench, roach, perch and rudd. In the district of Milgavie, there's both the Mugdock Park Pond and the Tench Pool. At Seafar, there's a carp pond and in the middle of Glasgow itself, there's Hogganfield Loch. This is a big water at eighty acres. It's very busy indeed and although night fishing is allowed I personally wouldn't advise it, considering some of the characters I've seen wandering around after closing time! The choice is yours. Still, there are carp reputed to be over twenty pounds in the water, along with some big bream and eels.

Just a little east of Glasgow you can find Lochend Loch in Coatbridge. This offers good perch and pike fishing and you pick up permits from the waterside. The Monklands District Coarse Angling Club now manages Monklands Canal just west of the town. This holds good bream up to six and even seven pounds, perch, carp, dace, rudd and tench. Day tickets only cost £1 and are available on the bank.

SEASON – coarse fishing is open all the year round in Scotland.

TICKETS – most of the waters are free or tickets can be bought on the bank. The best ports of call are the excellent Glasgow tackle shops. Try Tackle and Guns, 920 Pollokshaws Road, on 0141 632 2005; The Anglers Rendezvous, 74–78 Salt Market; or William Robertson and Co. Ltd., 61 Miller Street.

ACCOMMODATION – the Greater Glasgow and Clyde Valley Tourist Board, 11 George Square, Glasgow G2 1DY, on 0141 204 4400, can advise on accommodation.

LOCH LOMOND

Where do you start discussing a water that has threatened to make so much history over so many years? Of course, Lomond is considered by the Scots themselves as primarily a salmon and trout water, but the pike fishing, especially, is dramatic. There are perch and roach as well, so let's start by discussing those briefly.

Perch are widespread and roach seem to be more closely packed – you'll often find them in bays where rivers or streams enter. I'm not sure about the roach personally. Way back in the 70s I was tempted up on several trips by stories of three- and four-pounders that proved to be totally false. I, myself, have never contacted much over a pound and a half, although I can't say I've got to the bottom of Lomond roach stocks by any means. The perch certainly are larger. I believe they've been caught over four pounds in nets in the past, and further big ones are always on the cards. There are also powan – a freshwater herring – which are now under severe threat and fishing is closely controlled. Mind you, if you catch something strange on a single maggot and size eighteen when you're trying for a roach, at least now you'll know what it is!

So back to the pike. You've got to remember that Lomond is only just north of Glasgow and therefore, at the weekends and bank holidays especially, it is a real city playground. You'll find that most of the shoreline villages and marinas are a hive of activity at these times. But don't worry: at nearly twenty-three miles long and up to five miles wide, Lomond is a big enough water to get away from the crowds and do a great deal of exploration in near solitude.

Of course, you'll need a boat. It is possible to fish for pike from the bank, but it's an uphill task and you really can't cover even a fraction of a water of this magnitude unless you can get afloat.

In the bad old days, going back twenty years or so, Lomond was a Mecca for English anglers and they used to bring up huge numbers of their local live baits – ruffe, crucian carp, dace and so on. Not only was that inhumane, but it also caused great problems to the ecology of the loch itself. No more importing of live baits please! In fact, you'll find really that dead baits and lures do the business.

It's not a bad idea to troll with lures until you find you hit on the centre of activity. Just a pull or two should be enough to make you want to anchor up and explore the area more thoroughly. Of course, you can put a dead bait out and still work a lure in order to cover all options. The great key to success on Lomond really is location, so it does pay to cover water and, especially, to ask for local advice, which is generally freely given. An echo sounder is also a good idea to pinpoint drop-offs, underwater reefs and anything that could give a key to pike location. Also watch for fish striking. A pair of binoculars is a good idea. The important thing is not to be scared of the water, and approach it confidently, with as much advice as you can glean before setting out. Try to put aside a week or so, so that you can really get to know at least some of the loch.

In the springtime, many anglers go up to fish the spawning bays, knowing that the jacks will come in first and the really big mommas will be lying outside in deeper water waiting for their time to come. Of course, this is when you can fish from the bank in relatively shallow water, but it's still a good idea to have a boat close by so that you can fish the drop-off where the big females are likely to be most of the time. If you do adopt this approach, remember that pike are particularly vulnerable at this time of the year. They have spawning on their mind and it's not fair to interrupt them too much.

How big do the pike on Lomond really grow? Well, we know there are twenty-pounders aplenty and thirty-pounders are caught occasionally. The question really is how much bigger than that can get? There are all sorts of rumours. Fish on graphs recorders have been seen at great depths that have looked huge, but are they in fact a single fish or two or three fish together giving out an enormous signal? How about the pike that Fred Buller lost back in the 1960s, which Richard Walker put at sixty or seventy pounds? Naturally, the realists would say that with so much fishing pressure over at least the last quarter of a century a big fish – I mean a truly colossal fish – would have necessarily succumbed. Perhaps. Probably. But you never know, especially as Lomond pike fight like terriers. You've got to remember that if you've been used to lowland English pike, you'll find a quite different animal in the Scottish beast. They really go like wildfire. You sometimes just can't believe that it's 'only' a twelve- or a fifteen-pounder on the end of your line. If you'd lost that fish, you would have sworn that it was Fred Buller's sixty, alive and well after all these years!

☀ SEASON – you can pike fish year round.

🐟 TICKETS – the loch itself is under the control of the Loch Lomond Angling Improvement Association, c/o R A Clements and Co., 29 St. Vincent Place, Glasgow G1 2DT, on 0141 221 0068. It's a good idea to get in touch with them if you're planning a major campaign on the

The Llangollen Canal in Wales is a strange beast. You wouldn't really expect it to hold the calibre of fish it does, but there are some unexpected specimens along its short length.

A typical, small, chub river – the sort to be found throughout England, Wales and lowland Scotland. Chub are the canniest of fish so approach any swim with caution, especially one with little camouflage.

If you can't be on the river at dawn, make sure that you stay there until dusk! All fish become more active again once the light values begin to drop. This Wye barbel is giving a very good account of itself.

Loch Lomond offers tremendous possibilities for the coarse fisher. No-one really knows the pike potential – thirty-pounders are caught every year. There are also good perch and roach stocks.

A large, Scottish pike is returned to the water. Not a sight that every fly fisher would agree with, but there's a more enlightened policy these days towards returning the bigger fish, at least.

That Irish pike ace, Richie Johnson, is seen in action again. Richie is typical of his countrymen – he's charming, helpful and catches barrowloads of fish!

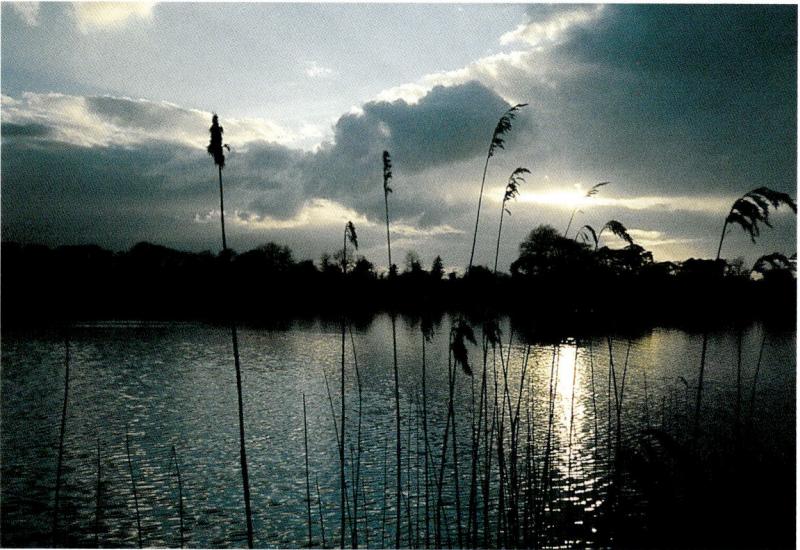

As the sun sets, surface activity rises to a crescendo. Tiny fish feed at the surface, predators are hunting, and bottom-feeding fish begin to get their heads down. Never be in too much of a hurry to leave.

❧ TROLLING FOR PIKE ❧

The pike fishing on the big Scottish lochs can be very rewarding and is one of the nation's best kept secrets. However, there are problems, not least of which is that of locating the fish, when you're talking about waters that can be miles long and hundreds of feet deep.

To get the best out of these lochs, you really have to go afloat and troll. Trolling is simply pulling lures or dead baits behind a moving boat.

These are potentially treacherous water, and safety is paramount, so that's where I'll start, with some simple do's and don'ts.

- *Always get an accurate weather forecast, and don't go out if heavy weather is expected during the day. It could come early and catch you out.*
- *Always wear a lifejacket.*
- *No matter how reliable your outboard motor is, always take oars and extra fuel.*
- *Always start out against the wind in case your motor fails. It's easier to row home with the wind behind you.*
- *Always make sure that somebody knows where you will be fishing and your likely time of return.*
- *Don't try to fish more than two rods when you first start out trolling, or big tangles can occur.*
- *It is a good idea to have a depth recorder with you to help you avoid sudden shoals or submerged islands.*
- *Start by fishing big, flashy plugs and spoons that pike can see down deep. A good vibration is also recommended, so that they can pick up on a lure they can't initially see. Start off with one deep-working lure and another that fishes higher in the water.*
- *Don't travel too slowly. A slow walking speed is about right for a kick off.*
- *Vary your course a bit and look for obvious hot spots such as islands, the mouths of bays or inflowing streams.*
- *If you hit a fish, put the engine into neutral and try to get your other rod in quickly. This will help avoid tangles.*
- *Always have an unhooking mat in the bottom of the boat.*
- *If you hit one fish, patrol the area carefully, as there are likely to be more pike about.*
- *Gear for trolling has to be tough and reliable. Rods of about nine feet in length are perfect and don't go for anything too expensive and fancy – if you're going to break a rod, it will be when you're trolling.*
- *Multiplier reels are perfect. A sturdy fixed-spool reel is fine, but a bait-runner facility is an advantage.*

water. Day tickets are not difficult to come by and are available at all local tackle shops, boat hire yards and hotels. You'll definitely need a boat, and the traditional centre has always been the boatyard in Balmaha.

➜ **DIRECTIONS** – Loch Lomond is northwest of Glasgow on the A82, which runs along the entire west bank.

ACCOMMODATION – there is a mass of accommodation ringing the banks of Lomond. There is everything from hotel accommodation to camping sites. Contact the Argyll, The Isles, Loch Lomond, Stirling and Trossachs Tourist Board, Dept. SUK, 7 Alexandra Parade, Dunoon, PA23 8AB, on 01369 701000.

LOCH AWE

Loch Awe, famous for its salmon and trout has also been a lure for serious predator men for at least a century! In Victorian times, it was the massive ferox trout – a huge cannibalistic brown trout – that drew the sportsmen so far north. In all probability, a monstrous fish of thirty-nine pounds was taken back in the 1880s, and since then there have been plenty of fish over twenty pounds recorded. These are magnificent creatures, and even though you're probably reading this for pike-fishing information, I'd urge you to take them on board and treat them very seriously. Of course, the bonus is that a massive predatorial brown trout is angled for in much the same way as a pike, so it's not exactly as though you've got to set your stall out for one or the other. No, you can fish Loch Awe pike-style in the secure knowledge that there's every chance one of these monsters could come along and make your angling life complete!

Awe is yet another huge Scottish loch and it is even more remote and, arguably, more inspiring than Lomond. There is no doubt that the ferox trout probably grow bigger in Awe than any other Scottish loch. So it occurs to me that the same could logically go for the pike. Pike fishing isn't over exploited, and that itself is a good sign: remember that pike thrive on neglect.

It doesn't matter which of these big Scottish lochs you are fishing, location is the key and, once again, you really will need a boat. These are easily obtainable from many centres, but do remember that when you're out on these very big waters you need to take every safety precaution. Mental attitude is almost as important as fishing ability. If you look at a water like Awe, Lomond or Ness and simply collapse within, then you're beaten already. You've got to tell yourself that there are plenty of pike, they are hungry fish, and that during the course of the day you're bound to cross the path of at least a few of them. Okay, these are big waters, but that just means that they have more fish in them. Keep your confidence high, keep working, and success beyond your wildest dreams could be the result.

I've fished Awe on dozens of occasions and, to tell the truth, have very frequently blanked. Mind you, there have been days when I haven't and they've been utterly splendid. My biggest ferox is a 'mere' ten pounds from Awe and I've only had pike nudging the twenty-pound mark, but I've seen much, much bigger. I was once up the northern arm where the River Awe itself runs into the loch. The water there is quite deep and crystal clear and I was fishing a dead brown trout, sink and draw. A pike – I thought it was a log at first – followed the bait in so close that I thought I'd be able to lift it out in a landing net. Of course, I couldn't: the pike was still deep down and it was vast. It would be unwise of me to put any weight on that fish because Scottish pike can be lean as well as mean. But, believe me, that was one big pike!

☀ SEASON – pike fishing is open all year.

✦ TICKETS – Loch Awe is protected and controlled by the Loch Awe Improvement Association and you have to have permits. These are available at most hotels and shops around the loch. Day ticket and weekly charges are modest. Contact D Wilson, Ardbrecknish House, Dalmally. Loch Awe Stores, Loch Awe, Dalmally BA33 1AQ, and any of the following hotels. You will need a boat, so contact the Taychreggan Hotel on 01866 833211. The owners have boats for the hotel's residents but also occasionally hire them out on a daily basis. The hotel, by the way, is absolutely excellent. Try also Cuil-na-sithe Hotel, on 01866 833234, or Portsonachan Hotel on 01866 833224. Contact also N. Clarke, 11 Dalavich, By Taynuilt, on 01866 844209.

→ DIRECTIONS – Loch Awe is situated on the A85 going west from Dalmally to Oban.

⊨ ACCOMMODATION – any of the hotels above offer splendid accommodation at differing rates. There is also a great deal of bed and breakfast and guesthouse accommodation around the loch. There are also some camp sites. The Argyll, the Isles, Loch Lomond, Stirling and Trossachs Tourist Board can give further advice and details on 01369 701000.

PIKE IN THE HIGHLAND LOCHS

This is a project for the fearless. Let's get it straight from the start, however, that I'm going to be talking about an area centred on Loch Ness that offers excellent holiday possibilities. This is the most wonderful countryside to explore with the whole family, and there is some charming accommodation available. Alternatively, for the single angler or party of piking pals, this area does offer a whole host of opportunities. And, you will be largely on your own. I've fished the area intensively for some fifteen years, but I don't pretend to know it well yet. In fact, when it comes to pike in general, I don't think there's anybody who truly does. Yes, I've had pike – good ones – and seen some monsters, but I'd never say it's easy fishing.

A real word of caution here. Remember that if you are going to take pike rods onto these waters you are stepping very much into the game fishing world. Do, therefore, behave with all consideration. If, for example, you are approached by a boat of salmon trollers then please do give way. If by chance you've strayed onto a bankside where you don't have permission to pike fish and you're challenged, please do explain the situation and be polite. Landowners will realise that mistakes are easily made providing you are not in anyway rude or aggressive. Don't leave any litter. Don't land a boat on bankside that is obviously anyone's private property. Always make every attempt to ensure that you have the correct permissions before setting out. Check also that Sunday fishing is permitted: in some areas it is still frowned upon. Don't just think that you can roll up to any water and launch your own boat. This is often not the case and it obviously raises local hackles. If you should hook a salmon on your pike spinners then return it. It's good to return them anyway, and if you don't have a ticket, it's a necessity.

Where do we begin? Loch Ness has some tremendous pike fishing on offer that is hardly ever tackled at all. Once again, this is best fished by boat, but I've always fancied Urquhart Bay near Drumnadrochit on the north bank. This is a shallow bay and it does attract numbers of prey fish. However, do check that you're not on prohibited territory. Ness looks forbidding, but isn't necessarily so. You can find quite fishable water not far from the margins and there are fish of thirty pounds plus in the water.

The whole Ness system is an exciting one. Moving south, you come to the much smaller Loch Oich. Now, a boat on Loch Oich really is an exciting prospect. This is predominantly a shallow loch and often quite weedy, and it has big pike stocks. Thirty-pounders are again present. Moving further south once more, we come to Loch Lochy, with some cracking fish available in the bays and on the extensive shallows. Neither should you ignore the stretches of Caledonian Canal that link the lochs together. The basins, in particular, can often provide dramatic sport.

There are rumours of big pike in some of the lochs to the south of the Ness system, for example Loch Duntelchaig, but I don't have personal experience of this water. I do know, however, the waters to the northwest. Loch Cluanie is a water with a big reputation and I know of at least one twenty-eight-pounder to come from it. Not bad when you consider how little piking pressure it receives. Some years there are pike matches on Loch Claunie and good fish are invariably taken – and this is from the bankside.

Moving further south, Loch Loyne is a mysterious, brooding sort of place. I have done well on Loyne, but to be honest it has been a struggle. I did see one enormous fish hooked, played to the surface and eventually lost down by the dam where it's possible to fish from the bank.

Loch Garry is a system that offers tremendous potential. Some four or five years ago, my fishing partner, Roger Miller, hooked a monstrous fish whilst spinning for char. He actually played it to the bank, but a group of Scottish fly fishermen appeared and began to start talking about killing the fish. Miller couldn't have that and pulled intentionally for a break, bless him. How big was that fish? Well, Roger has caught them to thirty–nine and a half pounds in England and guesses this fish was of the same ilk. I'm not surprised: a few years ago a couple of fish of forty pounds or more were taken by the nets of the local fishery management teams. And there is talk of a fifty-pounder that was caught some time back in the 1960s.

There are enormous fish certainly, and the potential in these farflung waters is colossal, but remember, you will be on your own. The chances of seeing other pike anglers are slim, so you've got to content yourself with what local advice you can glean and also explore off your own bat. No matter how 'piky' a place looks, if you don't get some action after a while, you've simply got to move on. Mobility is, as ever, the key.

☀ **SEASON –** the pike season here is, I suppose, officially year round, but in practical terms fishing from the end of October to the beginning of April is rarely possible. It would take a hard man to fish the winter through.

TICKETS – the pike fishing is generally free around the area and, indeed, many fishery owners will be only too pleased to let you pike fish providing you agree to take the small fish out. I don't think this is too much of a problem providing that everybody agrees that fish of twelve pounds or more go back in for the good of the trout fishing itself. Contact, J. Graham and Co., 37-39 Castle Street, Inverness on 01463 233178 for information about boats and access. Try also Frasers, 15 Market Arcade, Inverness IV1 1PG, on 01463 710929. The Foyers Hotel, on 01456 486216, offers boats halfway down the south bank and there are boatyards in Drumnadrochit. On Loch Oich, the Glengarry Castle Hotel, on 01809 501254, at Invergarry occasionally has rowing boats for hire. Moving onto the Garry system, the Tomdoun Hotel, on 01809 511244, offers boats on Garry itself and the shallow Inchlaggan Loch that adjoins it.

➔ **DIRECTIONS –** the Loch Ness system is situated on the A82 from Fort William to Inverness.

▭ **ACCOMMODATION –** the Tourist Information Centre in Inverness, on 01463 234353, can supply details of accommodation available in the area. Alternatively, contact the Highlands of Scotland Tourist Board, Peffrey House, Strathpeffer, Ross-shire IV14 9HA, on 0870 5143070. All the hotels mentioned are highly recommended, especially the Tomdoun, which I've known personally for many years.

GRAYLING FISHING ON THE RIVER TUMMEL

From 30th June to 14th March you are allowed to fish for grayling on the beautiful River Tummel with bait or fly, of course . This is a tremendous privilege, because the Tummel is a top salmon and trout river. Always remember this, and please defer to anglers who are spending almost ten times more on a day ticket than you are yourself. That said, there are large stretches of the Tummel available and you will be able to hide yourself away and enjoy some pretty solitary sport.

Tummel grayling always excite me. I've caught grayling all round the British Isles – and in many countries abroad come to that – but I've never found bigger, more solid-shouldered, more deeply-coloured fish than in the Tummel. They fight savagely, too, in the quick currents, and take bait with true ferocity. Mind you, they're not everywhere and you've got to spend time locating them. Ask for local knowledge and it will be readily given if politely requested. Trout anglers, for example, often know where shoals of grayling are hanging up. But failing that, you've got to do it on your own and this means travelling light and fishing as you go. Don't, therefore, encumber yourself with a lot of tackle. Rod, reel, floats, hooks, shot, bait and a small landing net, and off you go. Thigh boots at the very least will probably be necessary, and chest waders will give you better access to some of the swims. Don't discount any stretch of water. Sometimes it's tempting to say that a piece of river is just too fast-moving, but don't dismiss it. Okay, concentrate on the slower, more seductive areas, but everywhere deserves fishing.

As for bait, my two favourites would have to be small redworm or, interestingly enough, sweetcorn! In fact, come to think of it, I'd be quite happy just fishing sweetcorn all the time on the Tummel. I would certainly say that the majority of my fish have fallen to this bait. It's also an easy bait to procure in Scotland, which is more than can be said for many other coarse-fishing baits.

☀ SEASON – you can only fish for grayling with the fly before 30th June and from then on it's fly or bait right through to 14th March. There is no trout fishing between 7th October and 14th March, so apart from a few salmon fishermen, the grayling men will have the water to themselves.

✦ TICKETS – these cost £4 a day and are available from that excellent tackle shop, Mitchells of Pitlochry, 23 Athol Road, Pitlochry, on 01796 472613. Other information is also given by Ross Gardiner on 01796 472157 in the evenings. Ross is a magnificent grayling fisherman and a marvellous man. Only phone him please with very serious inquiries. Do make sure that you study the map before setting off to fish. Your ticket will cover several miles of water but there are stretches here and there that are out of bounds. Do not poach.

➡ DIRECTIONS – the River Tummel runs alongside a stretch of the A9 between Ballinluig and Pitlochry.

⊨ ACCOMMODATION – Pitlochry offers a whole array of accommodation from grand hotels down to homely bed and breakfasts. Contact the Perthshire Tourist Board, Lower City Mills, West Mill Street, Perth PH1 5QP, on 01738 627958.

❧ Highly Recommended Fisheries ❧

- *Castle Loch and Hightae Mill Loch, Loch Maben, Dumfries and Galloway. Contact the Warden, Loch Field, Loch Maben, Dumfries and Galloway. Both lochs offer excellent fishing for bream, carp, perch, tench and roach. Boat fishing only on Hightae Mill.*
- *Kelhead Quarry, Nr. Ecclefechan, Dumfries and Galloway. Good perch, roach, bream and pike. Some carp and tench. Phone 01461 700344.*
- *Strathclyde Country Park Loch. Close to the River Clyde. Carp, bream, roach, pike, perch and dace. Permits from the Booking Office, Strathclyde Country Park, Hamilton Road, Motherwell. Phone 01698 266155.*
- *Lochs Spectacle, Garwachie and Eldrig. All near Newton Stewart. Attractive lochs offering pike, perch, tench, roach and rudd in the main. Contact Newton Stewart Forest District Ranger on 01671 402420.*
- *Loch Ken, Dumfries and Galloway. Big pike, big roach and some good perch. Tickets available from local hotels and shops. A boat is advisable.*

Coarse-Fishing Sites in Ireland

1. Lough Mark
2. Lough Comb
3. Lough Key
4. Corrick and Shannon
5. Lough Ree
6. Athlone
7. Lough Dog
8. River Bann
9. Lower Lough Erne
10. Grand Canal
11. Lough Muckno
12. Upper River Bann
13. The River Erne
14. The River Blackwater
15. Lough Allen
16. Royal Canal
17. Lough Muck
18. Clay Lake

NORTHERN IRELAND

REPUBLIC OF IRELAND

‘*The more I catch, the more I realise I know next to nothing about pike fishing in this country. Each season I learn more about old waters and find so many new ones that you hardly know where to cast next. Only the other day I heard about a lough – a small one, virtually unfished – and it produced a thirty-four-pounder to the first guys to go there. Just like that. I could tell you similar stories for a week on end.*’

DAVID OVERY, IRISH WRITER AND PIKE LEGEND

D avid Overy is one of Ireland's best known, and certainly most successful, pike anglers, and I well remember this conversation with him over breakfast in one of Dublin's finest hotels.

It is no wonder that Ireland has drawn pike fishermen to its waters for well over a hundred years now. The great trout-rich loughs and bream-infested rivers have produced some of the world's biggest pike – and if you only half believe the legends, there are pike to put shark to shame! Of course, Ireland is a bit like that: it's a land of mists and magic, and there are times when you are afloat on a water like Mask or Corrib when you can believe that just about anything is underneath you. Mind you, you would probably be right!

Even if pike are not your thing, Ireland is still bound to have a huge amount to offer. The bream fishing is probably the best in the world. There are rudd to die for. Where else can you catch endless amounts of five- and six-pound tench from scores of waters that are all but virgin?

Ask anybody who has been over to Ireland with a fishing rod, and they will tell you there is a lot more to the country than just the sport itself. The Irish are themselves a revelation and make any journey a pleasure. You won't find a more genuine people anywhere. And after the day on the water, go into any pub, order a Guinness, let the bar know that you are a fisherman, and you'll be inundated with information. You will be told about waters that aren't even on maps, and they are bound to be full of fish. Quiet roads, sumptuous farmhouse breakfasts, waters with not a footprint beside them. Get yourself over there!

THE SHANNON

The Shannon is a magnificent and extraordinary watercourse. It's a hundred and sixty miles long with a catchment area that takes in the greater part of central Ireland. It's a limestone river, rich in weed and food, gently flowing for the most part, but with deep glides and, fascinatingly, an amazing number of loughs and lagoons off its spinal cord. To know the Shannon in a dozen lifetimes would be all but impossible. There's just so much water to fish, so much of it hidden and secretive, only accessible, naturally enough, by boat. The Irish themselves adore the Shannon. It's a constant magnet to them, and hardly surprising when you think of the huge number of specimen fish that it's produced over the decades. Pike, bream, rudd, perch – you name it, the Shannon holds it. So, in many ways, the Shannon is the core of coarse fishing throughout Ireland but, with my few attempts on the river, how could I possibly begin to describe it? I couldn't. Enter my dear friend from Dublin, Charlie Stuart – a man who's lived his leisure life on the great river.

'Let's take the northern area first, from Lough Key down to Carrick-on-Shannon. You could spend the best part of a year exploring this area, if not your entire life. The list of species to be caught is quite breathtaking, from the humble roach to regular catches of big double-figure pike. Let's start at **Lough Key** where you can gain access to the water by driving from Carrick towards Boyle in County Roscommon. About four miles outside Carrick ,you will come across Lough Key Forest Park, which in itself is a most beautiful spot to visit. If you enter the park ,you will see a large tower, below which are jetties. It's from these that I've had some of my best bream and perch fishing ever. Lough Key produced an Irish record pike tipping the scales at thirty-nine pounds and three ounces, so it's well worth a visit for big predators. The lake is easily accessible for pleasure craft, so you won't have any shortage of company – what I'm trying to say is that even though I've had bags of bream well over a hundred pounds, being a night owl helps. You'll find they tend to feed after midnight until four or five o'clock in the morning later on a dull day.

'Moving downstream, we'll come to the smaller water of **Oakport Lough**. It's situated behind the village of Knockvicar. It's a lake that's an absolute must for any keen piker. You'll find boat hire available locally in the village and the northern shore of this reed-lined water seems to produce the best fishing. The best methods by far are trolled or wobbled dead baits. As the lake is virtually inaccessible overland, you've got to organise boat hire in the village. Just ask at the bar and you'll be sent in the right direction.

A little further down the Shannon you will come across **Lough Drumharlow**. This is an ideal water for the general all rounder and the family on holiday. It produces bags of roach, tench and bream and, as you'd expect, significant numbers of good double-figure pike. The lake is accessible from the road but some anglers opt for the tranquillity of fishing from the island. Boat hire is essential to get you over and, once again, simply ask at that bar! I always say that the coarse fishing in Ireland is free but you've got to have a pound or two in your pocket for the odd Guinness!

'Having covered the local lakes of the northern section, I should add that there are sections of river here that are well worth a visit. Large areas of the banks are unfishable, but if you can get on the water, you will be surprised at the amazing clarity of the water, and you can actually see shoals of fish cruising along the riverbed. It's really brilliant to watch the bream and tench, moving slowly, tipping to feed, kicking up clouds of silt. It gets the heart beating, I can tell you. I should mention the area around Carrick-on-Shannon itself here. There are impressive bags of fish put together here, even in the harbour of the town centre, but the quality of the water does leave a lot to be desired and you won't get that clarity I was just talking about. Having said that, the town itself is well worth a visit after a session, because the hospitality and nightlife would rejuvenate the bones of the wettest fisherman!

'Moving down south from Carrick you enter a maze of waters that you could lose yourself in forever. The river splits in two directions, with the main section flowing through the settlement of Jamestown, while the other section is cut off through the Albert canal. The canal itself is not really worth a visit before reaching Albert Lough, due to the volume of boat traffic that passes along its length. Below Albert Lough, the canal rejoins the river to flow into **Lough Boderg**, which in turn flows into **Lough Bofinn**. It is at the meeting of these two waters that the river narrows. This is probably the best location on the two waters, as the shoreline is protected by a large forest, which gives you good shelter and comfortable fishing. The sport in this area is generally excellent, but be prepared to carry large amounts of ground bait – a good sharper would not go amiss! Bags include bream up to six pound plus and some pristine tench. Just north of Roosky is a beautiful village of **Dromod**. I've spent many a pleasant evening fishing in the harbour here, but again you have to be prepared to burn the midnight oil, as the place is very busy during the day. The fish move back at dusk and from about midnight onwards as things quieten down, large shoals of bream begin to reclaim the harbour as their own. Bags of over a hundred pounds are not uncommon and, with the added benefit of public lighting, you can fish and see what you're doing until the early hours.

'If we move on again south towards **Rooskey**, again we'll find a busy village for the boating fraternity. However, I would really recommend a visit to the lough here, as there is a lovely quiet backwater behind the lough keeper's cottage. I've caught some great perch here, many weighing over two pounds. If your preference is for quantity, then the shoals of roach and perch will keep you occupied for hours on end – a great place for the kids.

'Let's have a look at the middle Shannon now, the famous area around Athlone and Lough Ree. Many people have thought about writing a book on **Lough Ree** itself alone, but we'll have to content ourselves here with just a short introduction. On the northern end of the lake sits the town of Lanesborough – a place that in recent years has become a honey pot for visiting anglers. The main attraction is the location of the local power station with its outflow of warm water. To say that you have to be up early to have access to a swim would be an understatement – this is what we all know as a really serious hotspot! It seems that the fish are attracted to the warmer climate that the outflow brings and the anglers follow. Bags of even a hundred and fifty pounds plus are not unusual. You'll find roach, bream, roach/bream hybrids, tench, rudd and any amount of perch. It's well worth a visit but, as I've said, you've got to arrive early or you'll be disappointed.

❖ NIGHT FISHING BASICS ❖

Night fishing can sometimes give you the edge, especially during hot weather. However, it is a specialised technique, and following a few basic guidelines can help to make your expedition successful and safe.

* *Don't go on your own for your first few sessions, but choose to go along with a friend. It is even better if he or she has night-fishing experience.*
* *Don't night fish in water that you don't have any experience of first. Always visit the swim that you intend to visit at night during the daytime, so you can get the feel of it and note down any over-hanging trees or other possible problems after dark.*
* *Lay everything around you that you might need during the darkness whilst it is still light. Make sure there is an order to all this so you know exactly where you can lay your hands on things in the blackness.*
* *Always have one big torch for emergencies.*
* *Always take a small torch for the little fiddly jobs such as rebaiting.*
* *A headlamp like miners used to use is a good idea, especially when you're playing fish and you need both hands free.*
* *Always take plenty of warm clothes ,even if the day has been hot. Temperatures can plummet after dark.*
* *Take plenty of food and warm drinks. No alcohol!*
* *If you do a lot of night fishing, it is a good idea to make sure your torch is mid red rather than white light. This can be done by using a red bulb or by colouring the torch face with a red marker pen. Red light is less likely to scare fish and is kinder on the eyes.*
* *Things that go bump in the night. Remember that the strange wheezing that is coming from that nearby bush is more likely to be a hedgehog than a werewolf! The world can seem weird after dark, but there is always a rational explanation for everything.*

'Moving south on the lake down the eastern shoreline, you come across **Inny Bay**, where the River Inny itself enters the lake. This is a spot that has become renowned for massive shoals of bream. Indeed, one of my pals once said that he had to stop spinning for pike as he was foul-hooking so many bream. It's a must for the visiting angler if you have the nerve to put a really big bag together. On the opposite side of the lake you have **Hodson Bay**, another Mecca for big bream bags. There's a hotel just above the area and you can see people landing fish from the bar itself.

'Now, we're at **Shannonbridge**, about to move down to Lough Derg itself. Shannonbridge is a little village lying on the border of County Galway and even if it weren't for the brilliant fishing it would be well worth a visit for its history. The main street of the town crosses the river over an impressive nineteen-arch bridge – hence the name. Beside the bridge is a massive fortress built by the British during the Napoleonic Wars back in the early 19th century. From this building, you will be able to see most of the area that you'll want to fish. I personally have had many wonderful evenings fishing in Shannonbridge, but make a decision about what method you are going to use before you start.

'This is important, as different species abound in the area and the current tends to be a little faster on this stretch of the river. Trotting is a winner, but so is ledgering. I've had good bags of tench and bream, and endless amounts of roach and rudd. A little way downstream of the town you will come across a cutting that is used by boats navigating the river, and it's at the entrance of this cutting that I've had some of my best pike fishing in the area. Try a wobbled roach, drifting in and out of the current, and you can expect fish well into double figures.

'Now we're at Shannon harbour, which lies on the Grand Canal, just before its entrance to the river. Running alongside the canal is the **River Brosna**. I've had some really impressive fishing on this river just where it joins the main Shannon. In one session, for example, I caught nine pike to fourteen pounds, all falling to a float-fished dead rudd. I must hasten to remind you that live baiting on these waters is illegal. Moving downstream to the town of Banagher, you'll find a large harbour there and the river tends to pick up momentum. In fact, you've got really quite a strong current through the whole stretch. The banks around the town tend to be very difficult to fish because they're marshy, known locally as the Callows. However, below the town of Banagher you will come upon a large weir and lough known as **Meelick**. It's here that the fishing tends to become more comfortable and you'll find some well prepared swims on the western side of the river. If you read Fred Buller's Domesday Book of Pike you'll see that a fish of some sixty-nine inches in length was found dead here. The estimated weight was ninety pounds. I will leave that to your imagination and your scepticism, but remember that if you were to land a fish of half that weight you would hold the Irish record! It would beat the river record by over three pounds.

'The town of **Portumna** lies on the northern shores of Lough Derg and this stretch of water has produced some massive fish and excellent sport for visitors and locals alike. The river in the area of Portumna is known to be very deep and in winter this acts as a magnet to the pike. Let's move now into **Lough Derg**, which is awe-inspiring! There's so much water that you could spend a lifetime exploring. The massive lough is riddled with bays and islands, and my own advice is to search out secluded bays, bait up and wait for the bream to come in. Alternatively, pole quietly around in a small boat looking for the rudd shoals. I needn't say a word to you about the pike fishing. Just take one quick look at the Domesday Book and you will see that there are thirteen entries for Lough Derg alone.

'Leaving Lough Derg – if that's at all possible – you'll come to the villages of **Killaloe** and **O'Brien's Bridge**. These are both popular venues for the coarse angler and you'll find many visitors there. Well worth a visit.

'In short, I've spent so many weeks holiday cruising the Shannon that you'd think I'd know most of the watercourse. I don't. Every time I visit, I discover a new venue and it's like starting over afresh. In fact, I don't think there's anybody that could know the whole Shannon system. You could spend a lifetime on it and still not scratch the surface. Mind you, that doesn't mean to say that you have to be an expert to catch fish. You don't. You won't find better coarse fishing anywhere in Europe.'

 CONTACT – for angling information and guidance on angling services in the Shannon region contact Shannon Development, Shannon Town Centre, County Clare, on 00353 61361555. Garry Kenny, Palmerstown Stores, Portumna, on 00353 50941071, will advise on fishing in the northern Lough Derg area. At Shannonbridge, contact Dermot Killeen, Bar and Grocery, Main Street, on 00353 90574112. In Roosky, contact Key Enterprises and Lakeland Bait – both shops are easily found.

 ACCOMMODATION – for information, contact Limerick Tourist Board on 00353 61317522, or Athlone Tourist Board on 00353 90294630.

BREAM FISHING – RIVER BANN AND LOUGH ERNE

The bream fishing in Ireland is arguably the best that you'll find anywhere in the world. There are huge shoals of fish in an endless number of areas. Moreover, these are fish that are rarely pursued – you'll generally find the Irish only interested in things with an adipose fin on them!

However, even though this is breaming paradise, the fish don't give themselves up easily and you've got to work quite hard if you want to reap the ultimate harvest.

There are several rules. In the summer, you've got to think about fishing early and late, if not through the night. If the water is clear and the sun is bright, don't expect to catch a good number of fish. Then you've go to ground bait heavily. These are very big shoals and they're hungry fish. If you just put out half a pint of maggots you'll hold a shoal of bream for half a minute. The best plan is to work out an ambush area, feed heavily in the late afternoon and wait for the bream to move over it in the evening. The majority of bream in Ireland are uneducated when it comes to tackle but they do want a lot of food to go down over.

Bear in mind the weather conditions. Ireland can change dramatically from one moment to the next. If the winds are warm and wet from the southwest and the temperatures are mild, then you can expect to find bream in shallow water. If, however, there's a dip in water temperature, look for them in water of over ten feet deep.

When it comes to what you give the bream, think things out carefully. It's no good just ground baiting with a couple of pounds – you've really got to pile it in and, above all, you've got to mix things into the ground bait that will keep the fish interested. Casters are obviously good, but a gallon or so, which is what you'd need, does cost a fair amount. So also with chopped worms – a few pounds of those wouldn't go amiss either. Instead, try a dozen cans of sweetcorn, stewed wheat, pellets and so on. What you've got to do is to keep a shoal of bream, anything up to five hundred fish strong, interested for hours on end.

Remember that the bream are not tackle shy and you'll find that they fight much harder in Ireland than they do in England. This means that you can go comparatively heavy – think about a size twelve hook and main line of four or five pounds straight through. There's also the point that a big tench could come along at any moment as well.

All the usual techniques do well but probably most big bags are built up with a swim feeder. It makes sense to cast your feeder to the perimeter of activity. If you put it right in the centre of the shoal, not only do you run the risk of disturbing the fish, especially in shallow water, but you've also got to get the hooked bream out. Fishing the edges, you might not get a bite instantly, but you won't break the shoal up.

If you don't fancy the idea of fishing through the night – and if you're on a family holiday it's easy to see why not – try ground baiting at nine or ten o'clock in the evening. Put out a great number of small balls of bait and then return at first light – so not too much Guinness! With any luck at all you will find that the bream have moved in over the ground bait in the hours of darkness and they're still there – giving you three or four hours hectic sport before packing up for breakfast and spending a day out with the kids. A nice compromise.

In Northern Ireland, **Portglenone** on the lower River Bann in Antrim has become a top venue. You'll find eighty purpose-made fishing stands there all with good access.
✦ CONTACT – Smith's Tackle in Ballymoney, on 02827 664259.

Try also **Lower Lough Erne** at Trory, Fermanagh. This is excellent in the springtime when the water starts to warm up. There are several purpose-built concrete fishing stands, and you can catch fish here nicely on the waggler.
✦ CONTACT – Field and Stream in Enniskillen, on 02866 322114.

In the south, try **Ballycullian Lake**, Corrofin, Galway. A brilliant lake with big bays – a major venue for big bream. Fish to ten pounds. The Shannon Regional Fisheries Board has provided boat stands in several areas. Excellent.

☎ CONTACT – Shannon Regional Fisheries Board on 00353 656837675.

The **Grand Canal**, Edenderry, Offaly. The Grand Canal flows close to this town situated thirty miles west of Dublin. It is a coloured water with masses of bream and some carp.

☎ CONTACT – Padraic Kelly on 00353 40532071.

Lough Muckno, Castleblayney, Monaghan. This is a large lake with big bream stocks. Pre-baiting very important here.

☎ CONTACT – Jim Mc Mahon on 00353 429661714.

Remember that bream are very well spread throughout the entire island, both north and south. There are huge numbers of rivers, loughs and pools with bream fishing freely available. Remember the old advice: go into the bar and order a Guinness!

ROACH ON THE BLACKWATER, THE BANN AND THE ERNE

The roach fishing in Ireland has become a phenomenon. They've probably been present in the country for getting on a hundred and twenty years now, and have spread rapidly – partly through natural causes and sometimes because of anglers transporting them for live baits (but not now that live baiting in the south is illegal). What is certainly not in doubt is that roach have become an important part of the Irish angling touring scene and some of my own first trips to Ireland were superb for the brilliant roach fishing down in the Munster Blackwater. What fishing it was back in the 1970s – the great roach explosion in the Blackwater around the Moy and Cappoquin. In fact, the renowned bacon factory at Cappoquin was the centre of it all. Dreadful times! By that I mean the river there fished best when the pigs were brought in to be slaughtered. A pipe ran into the river with gallons of congealed blood washing away in the stream. The roach, sea trout and seagulls went barmy! I confess, to my horror these days, I joined in the glut and had many a roach to just about two pounds and some big, big dace.

On the Blackwater, you didn't have to fish in such appalling surroundings to catch big roach. They were, and are still, freely available. In fact, today, the roach have spread so widely it's not difficult to find them anywhere. Only last year I enjoyed some fantastic roach fishing in Northern Ireland, around **Enniskillen** on Upper Lough Erne. The roach just seemed to come and to come. Fish all the way up to a pound on float-fished maggots just tripping bottom. Tremendous fishing.

Remember that, by and large, the roach in Ireland are less tackle shy than those in England. You can't always get away with heavier tackle and certainly not crude bait presentation, but you can afford to scale up a little bit. Feeding, too, must be done more heavily. In England we're used to scattering a pinch of maggots every now and again: over in Ireland you've got to be bolder if you're going to hold a shoal.

Try the **Upper River Bann**, Portadown, Armagh. Portadown used to be the hotspot for huge roach catches and is now recovering well after a bit of a slump. Big bags of roach are still possible, and you can catch fish nudging the two pound mark – fish of a pound are not uncommon at all.

~ CONTACT – Premier Angling, Lurgan, on 02838 325204.

The **River Erne**, Enniskillen, Fermanagh, once rewrote the record books, and even today there is some magnificent fishing available in the area. It's a tremendous centre for all manner of species, but the roach fishing must be amongst the best in Europe. Plenty of fish, and some very big ones indeed. Local knowledge is important.

~ CONTACT – Field and Stream, Enniskillen, on 02866 322114.

Down in the south, it's difficult to beat the **River Blackwater** at **Fermoy** in County Cork. This is a big river, running through the town, and it's full of roach and dace. Look for swims around the main town bridge and the renowned hospital stretch. There's really good trotting here, providing you work at the swim with plenty of feed. Everybody is willing to give you advice here. It's a real magnet for anglers, and there are championship matches held. You might not catch the really big roach of yesteryear, but there'll be some cracking specimens amongst them.

~ CONTACT – Pat Barrie on 00353 2536187.

Don't be afraid to explore the entire Blackwater – Cappoquin still produces some brilliant roach. There are all sorts of access points along the river, a most attractive water and a roach fisherman's paradise.

PIKE ON THE LOUGHS AND THE RIVER SUCK

Pike fishing in Ireland is still absolutely remarkable, though there have been problems in the recent past. At one stage, a great number of anglers from continental Europe were visiting Ireland, catching sizeable pike and killing them to take home the heads as trophies. Fortunately, this practice has just about ceased. Another problem is that pike have been remorselessly culled in some of the premier trout waters. This is still going on to some degree, but increasingly there is an acceptance that big pike actually do a water good and it's the jacks that have to be removed.

137

Having said all that, Ireland remains a pike angler's dream. Pike have been resident in Ireland for about four hundred years or so, and they immediately found Irish waters to their liking. Pike thrive on neglect, and for many decades they were certainly neglected! When the Victorians began to fish for them in the late 19th century they found pike fishing beyond their wildest dreams. The pike grow particularly quickly in the limestone loughs – rich feed for trout and coarse fish means good growing conditions for the pike. Not only is there plenty of day-to-day food for pike in most Irish waters, but there are also added bonuses. There's no doubt that some of the huge pike in the past have benefited from runs of salmon, sea trout, eels and even shad. In short, Ireland has everything that big pike need: large, rich, under-pressured waters, full of nutritious prey fish.

Catching very big pike from Ireland is not always an easy job. On some of the really large waters such as Mask, Corrib, Derg, Ree and Neagh, location is always a problem. You can either go on local knowledge – generally very freely given in Ireland – or take an echo sounder with you. You'll often be able to locate shoals of prey fish by bream and roach, and you'll certainly be able to discover drop-offs, plateaux and any other obvious fish holding areas. On watercourses such as Lough Erne, location is a little easier – the pike tend to follow the big shoals of bream and roach and so a good starting place is where you find general pleasure anglers doing very well.

To fish Ireland successfully for pike you have to have mobility, and that almost always means a boat. Fortunately, every single village in Ireland next to a waterway is well geared up for this. What I have found, however, is that it sometimes pays to take your own engine across. Irish engines are not always as reliable as they should be!

You've got to remember that live baiting is banned in the south but that doesn't mean that your chances are restricted at all. Dead baiting works very well and most of the waters are clear enough to provide excellent lure fishing.

I recently enjoyed wonderful pike fishing over a three-day period on **Upper Lough Erne**, just south of Enniskillen. My very first cast with a gold Super Shad resulted in a twenty-five pound pike! Things don't get better than that. For the rest of the stay I continued to do well with big, flashy plugs. It was largely a case of moving slowly around the waterways, exploring with a plug and, when fish were found, anchoring up and putting out a couple of dead baits. The fish averaged a very high size – around twelve to fourteen pounds – and another couple of twenties came to the net. All the fish were in superb condition, and even though it was at the peak of the fishing season, we only saw two other pike anglers out over the weekend. That is piking in Ireland for you: you can find yourself on a magnificent water and be virtually alone.

My other major experiences of pike in Ireland have been on **Loughs Corrib and Mask** and the potential here is awesome. Netting has reduced numbers to some degree, but my own belief is that this has only pushed up the possible potential size. I don't think anybody who fishes these waters is in any doubt that forties and even fifties possibly exist. Mind you, fishing can be heart-breaking. Because there aren't many pike in the waters, it's difficult to build up a picture of their movements. You're very much alone. The best bet, in my opinion, is to explore as much water as possible with big spinners and plugs. Once again, when you've found fish, it pays to anchor up and investigate more thoroughly with dead baits. In very heavy weather it's possible to moor up behind the islands on the big loughs, put out a couple of dead baits and wait. This can be slow fishing, but when the float cocks and the line begins to pull out, your heart really is in your mouth. This could certainly be the fish of your dreams.

It is very difficult indeed to give precise locations for pike fishing. It is so widely available and people will help you in every single way they can. For anybody taking their car over to Ireland, it could well be that you'll be landing in Dublin. If that's the case, then Dave McBride is the perfect man to inspire you and set you on your way. He's a fund of information when it comes to all manner of pike fishing and general coarse fishing in Ireland.

CONTACT – Dave McBride, Clanbrassil Street, Dublin 2, on 00353 14530266.

One hot area is the River Suck around **Castlecoote** and **Athleague**, Roscommon. There are big bags of bream roach and hybrids, and these seem to attract large pike. In recent years there have been rumours of big thirties being caught – well worth checking out.

CONTACT – Mrs Holmes on 00353 4321491.

In the west, there is excellent fishing on **Loughs Corrib, Mask, Coolin and Nafooey**.

CONTACT – John O'Donnell on 00353 9246157 for information about boats in the area.

ACCOMMODATION – Fairhill Guesthouse, Clonbur, on 00353 9246176, accommodates anglers and arranges fishing trips with boatmen.

Cong is a fascinating area and offers excellent pike fishing.

CONTACT – Michael Ryan, River Lodge, Cong, on 00353 9246057, regarding boats. O'Connor's Tackle Shop in Cong also offers up-to-the-minute information.

Ballinrobe and **Tourmakready** are excellent centres on Lough Mask.

CONTACT – Dermot O'Connor's Tackle Shop on Main Street, Ballinrobe. There are centres for boat hire at Cushlough Pier, Rosshill Park and Cahir Pier. Contact also Derry Park Lodge Angling Centre, on 00353 9244081, at Tourmakready.

The **Erne system** offers extremely good piking.

CONTACT – Field and Stream, Enniskillen, on 02866 322114, offers excellent advice.

ACCOMMODATION – Rossahilly House, on 02866 322352, is an excellent guesthouse, right on the water and offering brilliant bream and pike fishing. Advice is freely given. There is also marvellous accommodation on Bell Isle just south of Enniskillen on Upper Lough Erne, and boats are available. Phone Bell Isle Estate, Lisbellaw, Enniskillen, County Fermanagh, on 02866 387231.

IRELAND

In Ireland it is so easy to get off the beaten track and try a totally new water. How about **Lough Arrow** in County Sligo? This is revered first and foremost as a big trout water, but there are also some excellent pike.

🦯 CONTACT – Stephanie and Robert Maloney at Arrow Lodge, Kilmactranny, Via Boyle, for details, on 00353 7966298.

TENCH, RUDD AND PERCH ON THE ROYAL CANAL AND THE RIVER INAGH

Most of the coarse fish species in Ireland were imported at some stage or another. Perch and pike probably arrived in the 16th and 17th centuries. Carp probably came across during the reign of James I, whereas roach were a fairly recent introduction – probably appearing in late Victorian times. Tench and rudd are no exception. It is probable that the tench came over with the carp, or possibly earlier when they were imported from monastic stew ponds. The belief is that rudd came over with bream, possibly around the time of the Norman Conquest. What is sure is that all species have done very well, tench and rudd in particular. The clear, pure, rich waters produce great specimens, and the rudd do grow large. Two-pounders are common and the tench average a high weight, in most places between four and six pounds. The colossal tench of the English gravel pit scene have not appeared but Ken Whelan in his excellent Angler in Ireland records a fish between eleven and twelve pounds from the river Suck.

Both species are spread thickly throughout the north and the south of the country and you don't have to be a fishing detective to find good sport in most localities. For kick off, once again we turn to Charlie Stuart for his own personal favourites.

'Tench fishing is probably the most exciting and frustrating of all the branches of angling that I know of. When things go well, however, you just do not ever pursue a more rewarding fish. I suppose some of my favourite venues are the canals of the Irish midlands, places where I've spent many an evening and early morning stalking the species. One of the great attractions of these canals is that there are so many stretches that have yet to be discovered. Truly there are places where no Irishman, let alone a visitor, has cast a bait. Let's look, though, at a few stretches along the **Royal Canal** that really are worth particular mention and have a good track record. The first one has to be the canal on the Dublin side of Mullingar. You'll find this stretch flowing along the side of the main road and the landmark to head for is Mary Lynch's pub and bed and breakfast – something of a draw for tench fishermen. Take a right turn at the pub and you travel alongside the canal for about half a mile. You'll find every yard is teaming with fish. There are huge shoals of roach and rudd that can prove difficult in clear water. But it's the tench that are really special. In the summer of 2000 I witnessed huge numbers of tench and their spawning ritual. I'll tell you this isn't a sight for the weak hearted. There were heaving masses of fish thrashing in the water, quite oblivious to my presence. It was pointless to take the rod out of the car but what a beautiful sight to behold.

'As any good tench fisherman knows, the best times for the canal are from dawn until about ten in the morning, and then late in the evening, from around eight o'clock until it is too dark to see a float. The most successful method I have found is to use a common earthworm tipped with a single red or white maggot. Many is the time I've fished alongside other anglers who have been using different baits, and whereas they've blanked, I've almost invariably had a few good fish. Float fishing works very well indeed, and you won't be in any doubt when the tench are in your swim because they really bubble like crazy things here. Darkness and you pack up and make the short walk back to Mary's for a pint of the 'black stuff' and a wholesome supper. And then it's upstairs to bed, in all probability your room being one of those that overlooks the canal itself. A fisherman's paradise.

'Another extremely good spot for tench fishing is **Lough Patrick** outside Multifarnham. This village is located between Mullingar and Edgeworthstown. The lough is easy to find and any of the locals will point you in the right direction. Boat

❧ CLEARWATER RUDD ❧

Ireland has many sparkling coarse fishing alternatives on offer but perhaps the most dramatic is the rudd fishing on the crystal-clear limestone loughs. Fishing for them, however, can be a frustrating business.

- *Take your time as you move around the water – you'll almost certainly need a boat and either oars or an electric engine will be necessary.*
- *Drift more than you row.*
- *Scan the water with binoculars, looking for any surface activity.*
- *Choose warm, bright, comparatively still days.*
- *Look for reedy bays, water lilies – anything that gives the flitting rudd shoals some sense of security.*
- *Drift pieces of floating bread downstream and watch through binoculars to see rising fish at distance.*
- *If fish are located, use three or four pound line, a size eight hook and either a big piece of flake or a piece of floating crust about the size of a fifty pence piece.*
- *Dunk both the flake or the crust to give added weight for casting distance.*
- *Either attach a small float or watch the line for a take.*
- *When a rudd is hooked, hustle it away from the rest of the shoal as quickly as possible. Release all fish caught immediately. Rudd are arguably the most beautiful fish in the British Isles and keep nets do absolutely nothing for their appearance.*

hire is available in Multifarnham itself and I'd really advise a visit if you're intending to travel to the area. My one word of advice is to bring along plenty of ground bait even though the lake itself is quite small. The fish need a little tempting to bring on the feed but, once you've cracked it, the rewards are endless.

'It is almost impossible knowing where to start giving advice on rudd venues. Rudd are almost everywhere. Perhaps they're at their best in the big, clear loughs, but you'll also find them in the Shannon, in the backwaters especially, and also in some of the rivers. The **River Inagh** in County Clare and the **Owenavorragh River** in County Wexford offer good sport. Once again, I'd advise going back to Mary Lynch's for some of the best rudd fishing sport that Ireland can offer. You'd be amazed at the number and size of the rudd that you can see there. Just to give you an example, I stopped over briefly one afternoon a couple of years back and caught four rudd, which weighed in jointly at over seven pounds! Not bad for about twenty minutes fishing.

'Before I go, John, I ought to say something about the perch in Ireland. Like rudd and tench and bream, you'll find them pretty well everywhere and there really are some cracking specimens. But let me give you this last little tip. The place is in the little Forest Park at **Deonadea** in County Kildare. This little pond was stocked by an enterprising individual some years ago and has since become a place that turns up some amazing fish considering the water is so small. It teems with roach and that is obviously why the perch grow so big. I myself have had them up to three and three-quarter pounds, and one large perch that I caught coughed up a half-digested roach. So I don't have to say any more about the staple diet of the fish here. It's a tremendous place to visit if you're on holiday in Dublin. The park lies about four miles outside the town of Clane ,which is only about twenty minutes drive from the city centre itself. The water is shallow and how I fish it is to bait heavily with maggots and work the roach up into a feeding frenzy. The big perch then move in and you can pick them up on lobworm or, inevitably, a small roach dead bait.'

❧ HIGHLY RECOMMENDED FISHERIES ❧

- *Lough Muck. A thirty-five acre lake that is rarely fished. Only twelve pegs and fishing boats available for hire. Excellent pike, roach and perch. Just outside Omagh. Contact Kenny Alcorn for day permits on 0288 224 2618.*
- *Clay Lake, Nr. Keady, County Armagh. A hundred and twenty acres. Pike, rudd and perch. Controlled by the Department of Agriculture.*

INDEX

⌒AUTHOR'S ACKNOWLEDGEMENTS

Thank you to Carol Selwyn for her unstinting efforts during the research, typing and checking of this book. A truly heroic effort. Thank you also to Daniela and Anne for checking the fine detail.

Thanks also to Matt Hayes for all manner of assistance over the years, as well as his friendship, and to Roger Wyndham Barnes for his generous advice on the Thames. Thank you to Martin Locke – even though we didn't get that book done, I still learnt a great deal, Martin. I would also like to thank Bernard Double and Frank Guttfield for getting me started nearly a quarter of a century ago back on Wilstone – magic days. Thank you, too, to David Judge who initiated me into the mysteries of the Greater London carp scene.

Thank you to a whole multitude of Norfolk-based anglers – Dave Plummer and Steve Harper, for example, who also provided perfect companionship in India on a memorable trip. Well done, too, to guys like Chris Turnbull and John Nunn who are helping preserve and improve what we have here. Thank you to Mike Smith for all his help with fishing, photographing and filming over the years, and also to David Cooper for many happy memories on Blickling Lake.

On the Wye, thanks to Mike Taylor for fifteen years of friendship and to Bob James and Pete Smith – for providing oases of calm in a mad angling world. Thank you to 'Woody' in Hereford for always greeting me with a smile and up to the minute advice. Thank you to Martin James who has always been there in times of crisis and always offered help whenever he's been able to give it.

Thank you to Christopher West and Ross Gardner for all their help with things Scottish, and to Maddie, the world's best fishing dog.

In Ireland, thank you indeed to David Overy and most especially my great friends Richie Johnston and Charlie Stuart. Time and time again their generosity and help have been invaluable.

Adult Acne

30 Days to Clear Skin

By Andrew Duguid